THE BEST OF THAI COOKING

THE BEST OF THAI COOKING

1st Printing 1987
2nd Printing 1988
3rd Printing 1988
4th Printing 1991
5th Printing 1993

Published in Great Britain by
CENTURION BOOKS LIMITED
52 George Street, London W1H 5RF

British Library Cataloguing in Publication Data
Amatyakul, Chalie
The Best of Thai Cooking
1 Food: Thai Dishes - Recipes
641 · 59593

ISBN: 0-948500-02-6

Book Design: Grapho Limited, Hong Kong
Photography: Benno Gross & Associates, Hong Kong.
Illustrations: Peter Jones

Printed in China by Twin Age Limited

THE BEST OF THAI COOKING

CHALIE AMATYAKUL

EDITED BY JOHN MITCHELL

CENTURION

Vegetables make up a large part of the average Thai diet and the early morning markets buzz with activity.

CONTENTS

*A papaya is just
one of many
fruits that lends
itself to the
appealing Thai
art of fruit
carving.*

Spices and herbs, carefully blended to bring out the best in fish, fowl and meat alike, play a much greater part in Thai cooking than in Western cuisines.

CURRY PASTES AND CONDIMENTS:

Most of the recipes in this edition include, as an integral part, the ingredients for their own spice paste. However, by making a quantity of paste in advance, considerable time will be saved when actually producing the meal. The paste may be stored, refrigerated, in an air-tight container for a few weeks.

The following are 'stock' recipes for two of Thailand's favourite curries and for four popular condiments.

GREEN CURRY PASTE

12 small green chillies
2 shallots
4 cloves garlic
30 mm (1½ inch) knob fresh Kha
(Siamese ginger)
4 coriander roots
2 stalks lemon grass
1 tsp chopped Kaffir lime peel
10 black peppercorns
½ tsp roasted coriander seeds
¼ tsp roasted cumin seeds
2 tsp shrimp paste
75 ml (3 fl oz) coconut oil

Chop the chillies, shallots, garlic, ginger, coriander roots and lemon grass and place in a mortar. Pound slightly, then add the lime peel, peppercorns, coriander seeds, cumin seeds and shrimp paste and pound until fairly smooth. Finally, add the coconut oil and blend thoroughly.

Note: As this curry is intended to be quite hot, it is suggested that the seeds in the chillies NOT be discarded. However, this decision depends solely on personal tastes, as does the variation, up or down, of the number of chillies used.

RED CURRY PASTE

12 dried red chillies
2 shallots
2 cloves garlic
15 mm (¾ inch) knob fresh Kha
(Siamese ginger)
15 mm (¾ inch) knob fresh ginger
2 coriander roots
2 stalks lemon grass
10 black peppercorns
¼ tsp coriander seeds
¼ tsp cumin seeds
¼ cinnamon powder
1 tsp turmeric powder
salt to taste
75 ml (3 fl oz) vegetable oil

Soak the chillies in warm water to soften. Chop the chillies, shallots, garlic, both gingers, coriander roots and lemon grass and place in a mortar. Pound slightly, then add the peppercorns, coriander seeds, cumin seeds, cinnamon, turmeric and salt. Pound until smooth, then add the vegetable oil and blend thoroughly.

CHILLI SAUCE

10 fresh red chillies
2 cloves garlic
4 peppercorns
2 tsp palm sugar
2 Tbsp fish sauce
4 Tbsp fresh lime juice *

Trim the chillies and remove the seeds and 'ribs'. Chop the chillies and garlic and place in a mortar, together with the peppercorns, sugar and fish sauce. Pound until smooth, then add the lime juice and stir to blend thoroughly.

*Substitute vinegar or tamarind water if preferred.

CHILLI 'JAM'

4 shallots
8 cloves garlic
8 fresh red chillies
75 ml (3 fl oz) vegetable oil
125 g (4 oz) dried shrimps
4 Tbsp palm sugar
2 Tbsp fish sauce

Chop the shallots, garlic and chillies and sauté in half the oil until crispy, then allow to cool before placing in a mortar. Soak the dried shrimps for a few minutes, then add to the mortar, together with the palm sugar and fish sauce. Pound until smooth, then stir-fry in the remaining oil and allow to cool before using. Store in an air-tight container if not using immediately.

SALTED EGGS

275 g (10 oz) coarse salt
2 litres cold water
8 eggs

Place the salt and water in a saucepan and bring to the boil. Stir until the salt has dissolved, then remove pan from heat and allow to cool. Place the eggs in a glass or earthenware container, cover completely with the brine and leave in a cool area for at least two weeks.

Note: This method of preserving eggs will harden the yolk so that it may be chopped and added to dishes, as occasionally called for in Thai recipes. However, if being used whole as in the following recipe the egg must be hard boiled in the usual way.

SALTED EGG DIP

4 small red chillies
2 cloves garlic
2 salted eggs, hard boiled
2 Tbsp palm sugar
2 Tbsp fish sauce
4 Tbsp fresh lime juice
2 Tbsp coconut oil

Place the chillies and garlic in a mortar and pound well. Shell the eggs, chop roughly and add to the mortar, together with the palm sugar. Continue to pound until the paste is smooth, then stir in the fish sauce and lime juice and blend thoroughly. Heat the oil in a pan and stir-fry the mixture for 2-3 minutes, then set aside to cook before serving.

SOUPS

Soup is a very significant part of a Thai's daily fare and consequently the cuisine boasts some of the most palate-pleasing flavours to be found anywhere. A bowl is served at almost every meal, regardless of the time of day, and is placed on the table alongside the other dishes to be enjoyed a little at a time, as and when each diner chooses. Most are clear, light and, certainly by Western standards, highly spiced.

However, the soups served throughout the day at roadside stalls are much more substantial and are almost a meal in themselves. These usually consist of noodles cooked in a spicy broth together with vegetables and chunks of meat or chicken and, inevitably topped with fresh chillies.

But without doubt the most famous soup (and perhaps, where most foreigners are concerned, the best known of all Thai dishes) is Tom Yaam Goong, a prawn soup, flavoured with many local favourites, such as lemon grass, chillies, Siamese ginger, coriander, basil leaves and fish sauce. While many cooks will have their own ideas about specific quantities, and the flavour may differ a little from one home to another, the unique 'hot and sour' quality of the soup will be ever-present.

TOM YAAM GOONG
(hot and sour prawn soup)

400 g (14 oz) medium-size prawns
3 stalks lemon grass
2 cloves garlic
2 tsp chopped coriander root
4 peppercorns
15 mm (½ inch) knob fresh Kha
(Siamese ginger)
2 fresh red chillies
4 small fresh green chillies
4 Kaffir lime leaves
75 ml (3 fl oz) vegetable oil
2 Tbsp fish sauce
2 Tbsp fresh lime juice
freshly shredded coriander leaves

Shell and de-vein the prawns, leaving the tails intact. Retain the heads and shells. Cut the lemon grass into short lengths, approximately 25 mm (1 inch) and pound slightly with the back of a knife. Place the garlic, coriander root and peppercorns in a mortar and pound into a smooth paste. Slice the ginger, cut the chillies into very tiny rings and shred the lime leaves. Heat the oil in a saucepan, add the prawn heads and shells and stir-fry for 3-4 minutes. Then, add 1.5 litres (2½ pints) water and bring to the boil. Cover the pan, reduce the heat and simmer for 10 minutes. Pour the stock through a fine strainer into a fresh saucepan and bring back to the boil. Stir in the spice-paste and add the lemon grass, ginger, lime leaves and prawns. Bring back to the boil and allow to cook for approximately 3 minutes, then add the fish sauce, lime juice and chillies. Stir to blend thoroughly, transfer to a steam boat with the chimney filled with red hot charcoal and garnish with fresly shredded coriander leaves.

TOM SOM PLA
(sour soup with fish and vegetables)

175 g (6 oz) fish fillets
¼ small white cabbage
75 g (3 oz) green beans
2 spring onions
2 shallots
15 mm (½ inch) knob fresh ginger
2 cloves garlic
2 tsp chopped coriander root
1 tsp shrimp paste
½ tsp turmeric powder
8 black peppercorns
¼ tsp salt
3 Tbsp vegetable oil
1.5 litres (2½ pints) clear fish stock
4 Tbsp tamarind water
2 Tbsp palm sugar
freshly shredded coriander leaves

Remove any skin from the fish and take care to ensure no small bones remain, then chop into small chunks. Shred the cabbage and slice the green beans and spring onions into 25 mm (1 inch) lengths. Finely chop the shallots, ginger and garlic and place in a mortar, together with the coriander root, shrimp paste, turmeric powder, peppercorns and salt, then pound into a smooth paste. Heat the oil in a deep saucepan, add the spice-paste and stir-fry for 4-5 minutes, then add the fish, fish stock, tamarind water and palm sugar and bring to the boil. Reduce the heat, cover the pan and simmer for 45 minutes, then add the cabbage, beans and spring onions and cook for a further 2-3 minutes. Transfer to a soup tureen and garnish with shredded coriander leaves.

TOM KHAO PLA
(seafood and rice soup)

8 mussels
8 clams
125 g (4 oz) small fresh shrimps
125 g (4 oz) fish fillets
1 clove garlic
15 mm (½ inch) knob fresh ginger
1 shallot
1 tsp chopped coriander root
4 Tbsp vegetable oil
2 litres (3¼ pints) clear fish stock
salt to taste
freshly ground black pepper
200 g (7 oz) long-grain rice
2 tsp fish sauce
freshly chopped coriander leaves

Scrub the mussels and clams and rinse in cold water. Place into a pan of rapidly boiling water until the shells open, discarding any that fail to do so. Discard shells. Blanch the shrimps in rapidly boiling water, then shell and de-vein. Cut the fish fillets into small bite-size pieces. Crush the garlic and finely chop the ginger, shallot and coriander root. Heat half the oil in a pan, add the garlic, ginger, shallot and coriander root and stir-fry for 3-4 minutes, then pour in the stock and bring to a rapid boil. Reduce the heat and simmer for 15 minutes, then pour the stock through a fine strainer into a fresh pan. Bring the stock back to the boil, add the seafood and season to taste with the salt and freshly ground black pepper. Reduce the heat and simmer until the seafood is cooked but remains firm, then transfer the seafood to a soup tureen and keep warm. Heat the remaining oil in a pan, add the rice and stir-fry for 2-3 minutes, then add the fish sauce, stir to blend thoroughly and continue to cook for a further minute. Then, pour the stock over the rice, cover the pan and cook slowly until the rice is tender. Finally, pour the rice and stock into the tureen, stir well and sprinkle the finely chopped coriander leaves on top.

TOM CHIN GOONG
(prawn ball soup)

225 g (8 oz) fresh prawns
1 clove garlic
½ tsp chopped coriander root
¼ tsp salt
freshly ground white pepper
1 egg, lightly whisked
2 tsp cornflour
6 dried black mushrooms
75 g (3 oz) bean curd
2 spring onions
1.5 litres (2½ pints) chicken stock
2 tsp fish sauce
freshly chopped coriander leaves

Shell and de-vein the prawns and pass through a fine mincer. Crush the garlic and coriander root and place in a mixing bowl, together with the prawns, salt, freshly ground white pepper, egg and cornflour. Mix well and form into small balls. Rinse the mushrooms under cool running water, then soak in a pan of warm water for 40 minutes. Remove and discard the hard stems and finely chop the caps. Slice the beancurd and cut the spring onions into 25 mm (1 inch) lengths. Pour the chicken stock into a deep saucepan, add the prawn balls and fish sauce and bring to the boil. Reduce the heat and simmer for 30 minutes, then add the mushroom and continue cooking for 10 minutes. Finally, add the bean curd and spring onion, stir well and cook for a further 2 minutes. Transfer to a soup tureen and garnish with freshly chopped coriander leaves.

GAENG SOM GOONG
(curried soup with prawns)

400 g (14 oz) fresh prawns
1/2 green papaya
125 g (4 oz) winged beans
50 g (2 oz) baby corn
8 dried red chillies
4 shallots
3 cloves garlic
25 mm (1 inch) knob fresh Kha
(Siamese ginger)
1 thin slice turmeric root
2 tsp chopped lemon grass
1/2 tsp chopped Kaffir lime rind
1 tsp shrimp paste
1.5 litres (2 1/2 pints) fish stock
3 Tbsp palm sugar
3 Tbsp fish sauce
3 Tbsp tamarind water
1 sprig Kaffir lime leaves

Shell and de-vein one-third of the prawns and pass through a fine mincer. Shell and de-vein the remaining prawns, leaving the tails intact. Cut the papaya into small, thin slices, slice the winged beans and cut the stems off the baby corn. Soak the chillies in warm water until soft, then slice. Chop the shallots, garlic, ginger and turmeric and place in a mortar together with the lemon grass, lime rind and shrimp paste, then pound into a smooth paste. Transfer the paste to a mixing bowl, add the minced prawns and blend well. Bring the stock to the boil in a deep saucepan, stir in the spice-paste and cook for 2 minutes. Add the papaya, beans and corn, then season with the sugar, fish sauce and tamarind water. Bring back to the boil and continue to cook over a moderate heat for 5 minutes, then add the prawns and cook for approximately 3 minutes. Transfer to a soup tureen and garnish with lime leaves.

GAI TOM KHA
(chicken and coconut soup)

225 g (8 oz) chicken meat
25 mm (1 inch) knob fresh Kha
(Siamese ginger)
6 cloves garlic
3 shallots
1 tsp chopped coriander root
2 stalks lemon grass
6 peppercorns
1 tsp red curry paste
5 small green chillies
6 Kaffir lime leaves
8 coriander leaves
550 ml (18 fl oz) thick coconut milk
550 ml (18 fl oz) thin coconut milk
3 Tbsp fish sauce
3 Tbsp fresh lime juice

Slice the chicken and ginger. Chop the garlic, shallots, coriander roots and lemon grass and place in a mortar, together with the peppercorns, curry paste and half the ginger, then pound until smooth. Crush the chillies and shred the lime and coriander leaves. Bring half the thick coconut milk to the boil, add the spice-paste and cook for 4-5 minutes. Then, add the chicken, remaining ginger and all the remaining coconut milk and bring back to the boil. Reduce the heat and allow to simmer until the chicken is tender, then add the fish sauce, lime juice and chillies. Stir and cook for a further minute, then transfer to a soup tureen and sprinkle the shredded leaves on top.

GAI TOM KHA *(CHICKEN AND COCONUT SOUP)*

TOM GAI PROONG
(spicy chicken soup)

325 g (12 oz) chicken meat
125 g (4 oz) chicken livers
¼ tsp salt
freshly ground black pepper
2 shallots
25 mm (1 inch) knob fresh ginger
2 stalks lemon grass
6 Kaffir lime leaves
1.25 litres (2 pints) chicken stock
2 tsp fresh lime juice

Seasoning Sauce:
3 red chillies
2 cloves garlic
2 Tbsp sugar
3 Tbsp fish sauce
125 ml (4 fl oz) fresh lime juice

Slice the chicken meat and liver into bite-size pieces and season with salt and freshly ground black pepper. Slice the shallots, ginger, and lemon grass and shred the lime leaves. Bring the stock to the boil, add all the ingredients, except the lime juice and cook until the meat is tender, approximately 20 minutes. Season with lime juice, stir and cook for a further minute, then transfer to a soup tureen and serve with the prepared seasoning sauce. To eat: add a small amount of the sauce to each individual bowl as desired.

To make the sauce: chop the chillies and garlic and place in a mortar together with the sugar and fish sauce, pound until smooth, then add the lime juice and stir to blend thoroughly.

GAENG RAWN
(clear soup of jelly noodles and vegetables)

225 g (8 oz) jelly noodles
5 dried black mushrooms
2 tsp dried spice flowers
150 g (5 oz) fresh pork
2 cloves garlic
1 tsp chopped coriander root
¼ tsp salt
4 black peppercorns
75 g (3 oz) bamboo shoots
4 spring onions
75 g (3 oz) bean curd
1.25 litres (2 pints) chicken stock
1 egg
freshly chopped coriander leaves

Soak the jelly noodles in warm water until soft, then drain and set aside. Rinse the mushrooms under cool running water for 1 minute, then soak in warm water for 40 minutes. Discard the hard stems and slice the caps. Soak the spice flowers in warm water until soft and drain well. Pass the pork through a fine mincer and place in a mixing bowl. Pound together the garlic, coriander root, salt and peppercorns until smooth, then add to the pork, blend thoroughly, and shape into small balls. Slice the bamboo shoots and spring onions and dice the beancurd. Pour the stock into a deep saucepan and bring to the boil. Add the meat balls, reduce the heat and simmer for 20 minutes, then add the noodles, mushrooms, spice flowers and bamboo shoots and continue to cook for another 15 minutes. Lightly whisk the egg and add to the stock, stirring continuously until the egg sets. Finally, stir in the beancurd and spring onion and cook for a further minute. Transfer to a soup tureen and garnish with the chopped coriander.

GAENG JUED
(consommé with stuffed mushrooms)

12 dried black mushrooms
125 g (4 oz) lean pork
2 tinned water chestnuts
1 clove garlic
2 spring onions
1 tsp chopped coriander root
1/2 tsp chopped coriander leaves
2 tsp light soya sauce
2 tsp rice wine
salt to taste
freshly ground white pepper
175 g (6 oz) water melon
1.25 litres (2 pints) chicken stock
1/2 tsp garlic oil
fresh coriander leaves

Soak the mushrooms in warm water for 40 minutes, then discard the hard stems. Pass the pork through a fine mincer into a large mixing bowl. Chop the water chestnuts and add to the pork. Chop the garlic and spring onion very finely and add these to the pork, together with the coriander root, chopped coriander leaves, soya sauce, wine, salt and freshly ground white pepper. Stir to blend thoroughly and, if necessary, add a little cold water to form a smooth paste. Fill the mushroom caps with this mixture and place in a steamer for 20 minutes. Cut the water melon into bite-size pieces and place in a soup tureen together with the stuffed mushrooms. Bring the stock to the boil and pour into the tureen. Sprinkle a little garlic oil on top of the soup and garnish with the fresh coriander leaves.

GAENG LIANG FUG THONG
(pumpkin and coconut soup)

325 g (12 oz) fresh pumpkin
2 tsp fresh lime juice
75 g (3 oz) dried shrimps
2 shallots
2 fresh red chillies
2 fresh green chillies
1 tsp shrimp paste
250 ml (9 fl oz) thick coconut milk
750 ml (1¼ pints) thin coconut milk
salt to taste
4 sweet basil leaves

Peel the pumpkin roughly, leaving a little peel attached to prevent the flesh breaking up during cooking. Sprinkle the lime juice over the pumpkin and set aside for 20 minutes. Place the dried shrimps, shallots, chillies and shrimp paste into a mortar and pound until smooth. Pour the thick coconut milk into a saucepan and bring to the boil. Immediately add the spice-paste and cook for 5 minutes, stirring continuously. Add the pumpkin, reduce heat and simmer for 10 minutes, then add half the thin coconut milk and season to taste with salt. Bring back to the boil and continue to cook until the pumpkin is tender but not soft. Finally, add the remaining coconut milk and the basil leaves, stir well, bring back to the boil and serve.

FISH & SEAFOOD

Fish play a most important role in the average Thai diet and local markets abound with the multifarious catches which arrive daily from the surrounding seas and great inland waterways. Such common varieties as bass, garoupa, flounder, mackerel and perch lie alongside the less familiar lizard fish (usually made into fish-balls and used in soups), triggerfish (best curried), tassel fish (held in high esteem by many Thais) and catfish (the best of which are found in fresh water and which, when smoked, flaked and deep-fried, make a very tasty snack to be enjoyed with an icy-cold glass of local beer). And added to this colourful and bountiful display are the many crustaceans, molluscs and other sea creatures, such as squid, eels and turtles.

The methods of preparation are almost as varied as the species and, while whole fish or fillets may be pan-fried, deep-fried, steamed, boiled, baked or grilled, the meat may just as often be cubed, minced, flaked, dried or salted and used in curries, soups, salads, sauces and flavour-adding side-dishes. Kapi, Nam Prik and Nam Pla, all made from dried shrimp and fish (see glossary), are essential to the local cuisine.

POO TOM GATHI
(casserole of mud crab and coconut milk)

4 mud crabs
2 tsp chopped coriander roots
4 cloves garlic
10 black peppercorns
2 shallots
4 small green chillies
4 stalks lemon grass
1 piece Kaffir lime peel
175 ml (6 fl oz) coconut cream
750 ml (1¼ pints) coconut milk
2 Tbsp fish sauce
2 Tbsp fresh lime juice
2 Tbsp palm sugar
shredded fresh red chillies

Clean and prepare the crabs and place in rapidly boiling water for 5 minutes. Drain well, then break off the claws and chop the bodies into bite-size pieces (smash the shells slightly to enable the meat to be more easily removed). Place the coriander roots, garlic and peppercorns in a mortar and pound into a smooth paste. Slice the shallots, chillies, lemon grass and lime peel. Pour the coconut cream into a deep saucepan, bring to the boil and stir in the spice-paste. Cook for 3 minutes, then add the shallots, chilli, lemon grass, lime peel and coconut milk and return to the boil. Add the crab, season with fish sauce, lime juice, palm sugar and continue to cook for 4-5 minutes. Transfer to a serving dish and garnish with shreds of fresh red chillies.

POO PAAD GARI
(curried crab)

4 crabs, approx 450 g (1 lb) each
4 fresh red chillies
1 large onion
2 cloves garlic
2 spring onions
oil for deep frying
2 Tbsp red curry paste
salt to taste
freshly ground black pepper
175 ml (6 fl oz) thick coconut milk
freshly chopped coriander leaves

Cook the crabs in rapidly boiling water for 3-4 minutes, then remove and chop into pieces. Cut the chillies into fine julienne strips and chop the onion, garlic and spring onions. Heat the oil in a wok until it is almost smoking, then add the pieces of crab and deep-fry for 5 minutes. Remove the crab from the oil, drain on kitchen paper and set aside. Pour away most of the oil, then add the chilli, onion and garlic to the wok and sauté for 3-4 minutes. Add the curry paste, salt and freshly ground black pepper and continue to cook for a further 2 minutes, stirring frequently. Pour in the coconut milk, stir to blend and bring to the boil. Reduce the heat, replace the pieces of crab and add the spring onion and allow to simmer for 5 minutes. Transfer to a serving dish and sprinkle the freshly chopped coriander on top.

GOONG POW NAM PLA WAAN
(lobster with sweet and sour dip)

1 fresh water lobster
salt to taste
freshly ground black pepper
3 Tbsp melted butter

Dip:
2 Tbsp palm sugar
2 Tbsp tamarind water
2 Tbsp fish sauce
1 tsp crisp-fried sliced shallot

Clean and prepare the lobster and cut in half. Season to taste with salt and freshly ground black pepper and brush with melted butter. Place under a moderate grill and cook for approximately 8 minutes, occasionally basting with the remaining butter. Transfer to a plate and serve with the dip.

To make the dip: place the palm sugar and tamarind water in a small saucepan over a low heat. Stir until the sugar has completely dissolved, then add the fish sauce. Continue to cook for a further minute, then transfer to a serving bowl and sprinkle the crispy-fried shallot on top.

GAENG GARI GOONG
(lobster and prawn curry)

4 fresh rock lobster tails
4 fresh tiger prawns
1 small green pepper
2 fresh red chillies
75 ml (3 fl oz) vegetable oil
3 Tbsp curry paste
2 Tbsp fish sauce
2 Tbsp sugar
8 cherry tomatoes
12 seeded red dates
250 ml (9 fl oz) thick coconut milk
freshly chopped coriander leaves

Carefully remove all the lobster meat and cut into slices. Shell and de-vein the prawns and cut in half lengthways. Cut the green pepper into small chunks and slice the chilli finely. Heat the oil in a large wok until it is very hot, then add the lobster and prawns and stir-fry for 2-3 minutes. Remove the seafood, drain on kitchen paper and set aside. Add the curry paste to the wok and cook for 3 minutes, stirring continuously, then add the fish sauce, sugar, pepper, chilli, tomatoes, dates and coconut milk. Stir well and bring to the boil, then replace the seafood, reduce the heat and cook slowly for 5-6 minutes, stirring occasionally. Transfer to a serving dish and sprinkle the freshly chopped coriander on top.

GAENG GARI GOONG *(LOBSTER AND PRAWN CURRY)*

POO JA
(stuffed crab shells)

4 medium-size crabs
125 g (4 oz) lean pork
1 small onion
2 cloves garlic
25 mm (1 inch) knob fresh ginger
1 tsp chopped coriander root
2 finely chopped coriander leaves
125 ml (4 fl oz) thick coconut milk
2 Tbsp cornflour
1 egg, lightly whisked
salt to taste
freshly ground black pepper
oil for deep frying

Cook the crabs in rapidly boiling water. Carefully remove the top shells and set these aside. Extract all the meat from the body and claws and shred finely. Chop the pork very finely or pass through a mincer. Chop the onion, garlic and ginger. Place all the ingredients in a bowl and mix thoroughly. Transfer the mixture into the crab shells and place in a steamer for 30 minutes. Remove, set aside and allow to cool. Just prior to serving, heat the oil until it begins to smoke, then deep-fry the stuffed shells for 2 minutes, until the top is a golden brown.

POO JA *(STUFFED CRAB SHELLS)*

GAENG KHIAW WAAN GOONG
(green curry with prawns)

675 g (1½ lbs) fresh prawns
2 shallots
4 cloves garlic
25 mm (1 inch) knob fresh Kha (Siamese ginger)
3 coriander roots
8 fresh red chillies
4 small green chillies
2 stalks lemon grass
2 tsp chopped Kaffir lime peel
10 black peppercorns
1 tsp coriander seeds
2 tsp cumin seeds
½ tsp turmeric powder
1 tsp shrimp paste
4 basil leaves
4 Kaffir lime leaves
125 ml (4 fl oz) coconut cream
350 ml (12 fl oz) thick coconut milk
2 Tbsp fish sauce
2 tsp palm sugar
fresh coriander leaves

Shell and de-vein the prawns, then wash, pat dry and set aside. Chop the shallots, garlic, ginger, coriander roots, chillies and lemon grass and place in a mortar. Pound slightly, then add the lime peel, peppercorns, coriander seeds, cumin seeds, turmeric powder and shrimp paste and continue pounding until smooth. Shred the basil and lime leaves. Pour the coconut cream into a wok, bring to the boil and stir continuously until the oil rises to the surface. Then, add the spice-paste and continue to stir, over a moderately-hot heat until the mixture is thick and fragrant. Add the prawns and one third of the coconut milk and bring back to the boil. Gradually stir in all the remaining milk, then add the basil and lime leaves. Cook until the liquid has reduced by one third, then add the fish sauce and sugar and stir to blend thoroughly. Transfer to a serving bowl and garnish with fresh coriander leaves.

GAENG KHIAW WAAN GOONG *(GREEN CURRY WITH PRAWNS)*

TOD MAN PLA
(fried prawn cakes with hot sauce)

675 g (1¹/₂ lbs) fresh prawns
125 g (4 oz) long green beans
2 tsp red chilli paste
2 tsp light soya sauce
4 Tbsp thick coconut milk
1 egg
2 Tbsp cornflour
salt to taste
freshly ground black pepper
75 ml (3 fl oz) vegetable oil
tomato wedges
cucumber wedges

Hot Sauce:
2 fresh red chillies
1 clove garlic
15 mm (¹/₂ inch) knob fresh ginger
25 mm (1 inch) piece cucumber
1 tsp chopped coriander root
2 Tbsp crushed roasted peanuts
2 Tbsp sugar
2 Tbsp fresh lime juice
2 Tbsp light soya sauce
4 Tbsp chicken stock

Cook the prawns in rapidly boiling water, shell and de-vein and chop finely. Chop the beans into tiny pieces. Place the prawns into a mixing bowl, add the chilli paste, soya sauce and coconut milk and mix well. Lightly whisk the egg with the cornflour and add to the prawns, then add the beans and season with salt and freshly ground black pepper. Stir to combine the mixture thoroughly, then shape into small patties. Heat the oil and fry the prawn patties, turning once so that they are crispy and golden-brown on both sides. Arrange on a serving plate, spoon a little sauce on top and garnish with tomato and cucumber wedges.

To make the sauce: chop the chillies, garlic, ginger and cucumber into very tiny pieces and place into a mixing bowl, together with the coriander root and crushed peanuts. Dissolve the sugar in the lime juice and add to the bowl, together with the soya sauce and chicken stock, then stir to blend thoroughly.

PRATAAD LOM
(prawn rolls)

20 medium-size fresh prawns
1 tsp crushed coriander root
1 tsp crushed garlic
8 black peppercorns
3 Tbsp fish sauce
20 thin soya bean crêpes
oil for deep frying

Shell and de-vein the prawns leaving the tails intact and place in a shallow dish. Pound the coriander root, garlic and peppercorns in a mortar until smooth, then add the fish sauce and stir to blend. Pour the paste over the prawns and allow to marinate for 5 minutes, turning once to ensure an even coating. Wrap each prawn in a crepe and moisten the edges with a little water to seal. Heat the oil in a wok until it starts to smoke and deep-fry the prawns until golden brown. Drain on kitchen paper and serve with a choice of dips, such as plain soya sauce, chilli sauce or plum sauce.

PAAD PRIEW WAN GOONG
(sweet and sour shrimps)

675 g (1½ lbs) fresh shrimps
¼ tsp salt
freshly ground white pepper
2 tsp granulated sugar
2 Tbsp fresh lime juice
2 Tbsp rice wine
1 clove garlic
1 large onion
1 green pepper
2 tomatoes
½ small cucumber
4 Tbsp vegetable oil
2 tsp palm sugar
2 Tbsp tomato paste
2 tsp fish sauce
2 Tbsp light soya sauce
75 ml (3 fl oz) chicken stock
75 g (3 oz) tinned pineapple pieces
2 tsp cornflour
freshly chopped coriander leaves

Shell and de-vein the shrimps and place in a shallow bowl. Season with salt and freshly ground white pepper and sprinkle the sugar on top. Pour half the lime juice and rice wine over the shrimps and set to one side for 15 minutes. Mince the garlic and chop the onion, green pepper, tomatoes and cucumber. Heat the oil in a large wok and sauté the garlic and onion for 2-3 minutes, until the onion is soft and translucent. Add the shrimps and stir-fry for 3 minutes, then add the green pepper, tomato, cucumber, palm sugar, tomato paste, fish sauce, soya sauce, stock, remaining lime juice and wine. Stir well and bring to the boil, then reduce the heat, add the pineapple pieces and cook over a moderate heat for a further 3-4 minutes. Finally, mix the cornflour with a small quantity of cold water, add to the sauce and stir to thicken slightly. Transfer to a serving dish and sprinkle the finely chopped coriander leaves on top.

GOONG PAAD
(fried prawns with chilli paste)

675 g (1½ lbs) fresh prawns
1 shallot
1 clove garlic
25 mm (1 inch) knob fresh ginger
2 fresh red chillies
2 tsp chopped lemon grass
1 tsp chopped coriander root
¼ teaspoon chopped nutmeg
1 tsp shrimp paste
2 tsp fresh lime juice
175 ml (6 oz) thick coconut milk
salt to taste
freshly ground black pepper
125 g (4 oz) rice flour
oil for deep frying

Shell and de-vein the prawns, leaving the tails intact. Chop the shallot, garlic, ginger and chillies and place in a large bowl. Add the lemon grass, coriander, nutmeg, shrimp paste, lime juice and coconut milk, season with salt and freshly ground black pepper, then stir to blend thoroughly. Place the prawns in the spice-marinade, stir well and set aside for 30 minutes, then remove the prawns, drain well and dust with the rice flour. Heat the oil in a wok until it starts to smoke, then add the prawns and cook for 1-2 minutes until they curl. Drain the prawns on kitchen paper to remove excess oil before serving.

GOONG PAAD *(FRIED PRAWNS WITH CHILLI PASTE)*

KHAI JIAW HOY NAANG ROM
(oyster omelette)

275 g (10 oz) small oysters
freshly ground black pepper
1 shallot
1 clove garlic
1 spring onion
3 Tbsp rice flour
¼ tsp salt
3 eggs
4 Tbsp coconut oil
½ tsp finely chopped coriander leaves
shredded fresh red chilli

Wash the oysters under cold running water and drain well, then season with freshly ground black pepper. Slice the shallot, garlic and spring onion very finely. Place the flour into a mixing bowl, add the salt and about 125 ml (4 fl oz) of warm water and mix to produce a thin batter. In a separate bowl beat the eggs lightly. Heat the oil in a heavy-based frying pan and pour in the batter. Twist the pan so that the batter spreads evenly, then add the oysters, shallot, garlic, onion and coriander leaves and cook over a moderate heat for 1-2 minutes. Add the egg to the pan and continue to cook until the egg sets, using a spatula to break up the mixture. To serve: transfer to a serving plate and garnish with shreds of fresh red chilli.

HOY LAI PAAD HOR
(stir-fried clams with basil leaves)

675 g (1½ lbs) clams
4 cloves garlic
4 small green chillies
250 ml (9 fl oz) vegetable oil
20 fresh basil leaves
3 Tbsp fish sauce
shredded fresh red chilli

Scrub the clams with a stiff brush and rinse under cold running water, then place into a pan of rapidly boiling water and cook until the shells open, discarding any that fail to do so. Remove the clams from the shells and set aside. Crush the garlic and chop and lightly pound the chillies. Heat one third of the oil in a wok, add the garlic and chilli and sauté for 2 minutes then add the clams and halt the basic leaves and retain over a moderate heat for 2-3 minutes, stirring frequently. Add the fish sauce and stir to blend, then remove the clams with a slotted spoon and arrange on a serving plate. Pour the remaining oil into the wok and place over a high heat until it starts to smoke, then deep-fry the remaining basil leaves until crispy. Remove the leaves from the oil, drain well, then arrange over the clams and, finally garnish with shreds of fresh red chilli.

HOY LAI PAAD PRIG
(clams with hot sauce)

675 g (1½ lbs) clams
2 shallots
25 mm (1 inch) knob fresh ginger
4 fresh red chillies
1 clove garlic
3 Tbsp vegetable oil
1 tsp chopped coriander root
2 tsp fish sauce
2 Tbsp chilli sauce
300 ml (10 fl oz) fish stock
2 Tbsp cornflour
salt to taste
freshly ground black pepper
fresh coriander leaves

Scrub the clams with a stiff wire brush and rinse well in cold water. Chop the shallots, ginger, chillies and garlic. Heat the oil in a wok, add the shallot, ginger and garlic and sauté for 3-4 minutes, then add the chillies, coriander root, fish sauce and chilli sauce. Cook over a moderate heat for 2 minutes, then add the clams and fish stock and bring to the boil. Cook until all the clams open (discarding any that fail to do so), then transfer the clams to a serving dish. Mix the cornflour with a small quantity of cold water and add to the remaining stock. Season to taste with salt and freshly ground black pepper and stir well until the sauce thickens. Pour over the clams and garnish with coriander leaves.

HOY MALAENG POO LAAM
(curried mussels in bamboo tubes)

675 g (1½ lbs) mussels
125 g (4 oz) cooked crabmeat
bamboo tubes, approx 20 cm (8 inch)
125 g (4 oz) cooked white fish fillets
1 tsp shredded Kaffir lime leaves
1 tsp shredded balsam leaves
2 Tbsp chilli paste
2 Tbsp palm sugar
¼ teaspoon salt
6 eggs, lightly whisked
3 Tbsp fish sauce
175 ml (6 fl oz) coconut cream

Scrub the mussels with a stiff wire brush and wash with salted cold water. Cook the mussels in rapidly boiling water until they open, discarding any that fail to do so, then remove and discard the shells. Place the mussels and crabmeat through a coarse grinder and set aside. Halve the bamboo tubes and clean with salted water. Chop the fish fillets very finely and place in a mixing bowl, together with the shredded leaves, chilli paste, sugar, salt, eggs, fish sauce and all but 2 Tbsp coconut cream and stir. Add the mussel and crabmeat mixture and blend thoroughly. Then, spoon the mixture into the pieces of bamboo and top with the remaining coconut cream. Cover with a piece of aluminium and cook under a moderately hot grill for 20 minutes, then remove the cover and continue to cook until the mixture is set and the top is golden.

PO TAEK
(sour seafood pot)

8 fresh mussels
1 small crab
4 large fresh prawns
1 small squid
150 g (6 oz) sea bass fillets
1.25 litres (2 pints) chicken stock
2 pickled plums
3 Tbsp fish sauce
salt to taste
freshly ground white pepper
5 small fresh red chillies
2 Tbsp fresh lime juice
freshly chopped coriander leaves

Scrub the mussels with a stiff wire brush and rinse in salted cold water. Cook the crab in rapidly boiling water for 2 minutes, then cut into 4 pieces. Shell and de-vein the prawns, leaving the tails intact. Clean the squid and cut into 4 pieces. Cut the sea bass into bite-size pieces. Pour the chicken stock into a large clay pot and bring to the boil. Add the pickled plums, with juice, the fish sauce, salt and freshly ground white pepper. Reduce the heat and simmer gently for 10 minutes, then add all the seafood. Smash the chillies with the back of a knife and add to the stock, together with the lime juice. Retain over a moderate heat until all the seafood is completely cooked (discarding any mussels that fail to open), then garnish with the freshly chopped coriander leaves and serve.

HAW MOG HOY
(spicy steamed mussels)

900 g (2 lbs) fresh mussels
1 shallot
1 clove garlic
4 fresh red chillies
3 Tbsp vegetable oil
1 tsp chopped coriander root
1 tsp chopped Kha (Siamese ginger)
1 tsp chopped lemon grass
1/2 tsp chopped lime peel
2 tsp shrimp paste
175 ml (6 fl oz) coconut cream
1 egg, lightly whisked
2 Tbsp rice flour
salt to taste
freshly ground black pepper
sweet basil leaves

Scrub the mussels with a stiff wire brush and rinse in salted cold water. Cook in a steamer until they open, discarding any that fail to do so. Remove the mussels from the shells, retaining the larger shells. Chop the shallot, garlic and chillies. Heat the oil in a pan and sauté the shallot and garlic for 3-4 minutes, then add the chillies, coriander, ginger, lemon grass, lime peel and shrimp paste. Continue to cook, stirring frequently, until the mixture gives off a fragrant aroma, then remove from the pan and place in a mixing bowl. Add the coconut cream, egg, flour, salt and freshly ground black pepper and stir to combine thoroughly. To serve: blanch the basil leaves in boiling water and arrange in the bottom of the retained shells. Place 3 mussels in each shell and spoon a little sauce on top of each. Place in a steamer and cook until heated through, then serve immediately.

PO TAEG *(SOUR SEAFOOD POT)*

PLA MUEG PAAD PRIG
(fried squid with hot sauce)

450 g (1 lb) fresh squid
2 shallots
2 cloves garlic
2 fresh red chillies
2 spring onions
3 Tbsp vegetable oil
2 tsp fish sauce
2 tsp oyster sauce
3 Tbsp rice wine
salt to taste
freshly ground black pepper
freshly chopped coriander leaves

Prepare the squid and cut into bite-size pieces. Par-boil for 5 minutes, then set aside to drain thoroughly. Chop the shallots, garlic, chillies and spring onions. Heat the oil in a wok and sauté the shallot and garlic until golden brown and crispy, then add the squid, chilli, onion, fish sauce, oyster sauce and wine and season to taste with salt and freshly ground black pepper. Stir-fry over a moderate heat until the squid is fully cooked, approximately 8-10 minutes. Add the chopped coriander leaves, stir for a further minute and transfer to a serving dish.

PLA GRAPONG THOD FOO
(fluffy crisp fried snapper)

1 red snapper, approx 675 g (1½ lbs)
banana leaves
oil for deep frying

Clean and prepare the fish, then wrap the fish up tightly in the banana leaf and grill over a charcoal fire for approximately 20 minutes, turning once. Unwrap the fish and carefully remove all the bones and flake the meat. Place on a wooden board and pound the meat to an even texture, then spread out in a thin layer and allow to dry for 30 minutes. Heat the oil in a large wok and cook until fluffy and crisp. Remove the fish with a slotted spoon, drain on kitchen paper and serve.

PLA DOOK FOO
(deep fried smoked catfish)

1 smoked catfish
2 Tbsp fresh lime juice
1 tsp granulated sugar
freshly ground black pepper
oil for deep frying
banana leaves
shredded fresh red chilli

Take care to remove the skin and all the bones from the fish, then flake the meat, season with lime juice, sugar and freshly ground black pepper and place in a frying basket. Heat the oil in a pan until it starts to smoke, then deep-fry the fish until it is crispy and golden brown. Remove from the oil, drain on kitchen paper, then transfer to a serving plate covered with banana leaves and garnish with shreds of fresh red chilli.

PLA KAPONG PRIAW
(snapper in sour sauce)

400 g (14 oz) snapper fillets
salt to taste
freshly ground black pepper
2 shallots
4 cloves garlic
20 mm (¾ inch) knob fresh ginger
4 Tbsp vegetable oil
2 Tbsp dark soya sauce
2 Tbsp fish sauce
4 Tbsp tamarind water
2 Tbsp palm sugar
fresh coriander leaves
shredded red chillies

Cut the fish fillets into serving-size pieces and season with salt and freshly ground black pepper. Finely chop the shallots, garlic and ginger. Heat the oil in a pan and sauté the shallot, garlic and ginger for 2-3 minutes, then add the pieces of fish and cook over a moderate heat for approximately 6 minutes. Remove the fish, drain on kitchen paper and transfer to a serving plate, then add the soya sauce, fish sauce, tamarind water, palm sugar and stir until the sugar has completely dissolved. Adjust seasonings to taste, then pour the sauce over the fish and garnish with coriander leaves and red chillies.

NGOB PLA HAW
(baked curried fish fillet)

4 fish fillets, approx 150 g (5 oz) each
salt to taste
freshly ground black pepper
6 dried red chillies
1 shallot
2 cloves garlic
25 mm (1 inch) knob fresh ginger
6 coriander roots
2 stalks lemon grass
1 tsp shredded Kaffir lime peel
200 g (7 oz) grated coconut
1 tsp palm sugar
1 tsp shrimp paste
2 Tbsp fish sauce
75 ml (3 fl oz) vegetable oil
4 banana leaf wrappers
2 tsp shredded basil leaves
2 tsp shredded Kaffir lime leaves
2 tsp shredded fresh red chilli

Season the fish with salt and pepper. Soak the chillies in warm water for 15 minutes and drain. Finely chop the chillies, shallot, garlic, ginger, coriander roots, lemon grass and place in a mortar. Add the lime peel, grated coconut, sugar, shrimp paste and fish sauce and pound until smooth. Heat the oil in a pan, fry the fish fillets for 4-5 minutes, until three-quarters cooked, then remove and drain on kitchen paper. Spread a thin layer of spice-paste in the centre of each banana leaf wrapper and place a fish fillet on top. Then, coat the fish with another layer of paste and sprinkle the shredded leaves and chilli shreds on top. Fold the banana leaves and secure with toothpicks to ensure the cooking liquids do not escape, then place over a charcoal fire and cook for approximately 20 minutes, turning once.

PLA GOW LAAD PRIG
(fried garoupa with chilli sauce)

1 garoupa, approx 675 g (1½ lbs)
3 fresh red chillies
3 fresh green chillies
25 mm (1 inch) knob fresh ginger
3 shallots
2 cloves garlic
½ tsp chopped coriander root
6 white peppercorns
oil for deep frying
2 Tbsp fish sauce
3 Tbsp tamarind water
3 Tbsp palm sugar
75 ml (3 fl oz) thick coconut milk

Clean and prepare the fish, leaving the head and tail intact. Chop the chillies, ginger, shallots and garlic and place in a mortar, together with the coriander root, peppercorns and pound into a smooth paste adding a few drops of water if necessary. Heat the oil in a pan until it starts to smoke, then deep-fry the fish until it is cooked and the skin is golden and crispy. Remove the fish from the oil, drain on kitchen paper and arrange on a serving dish, then set aside and keep warm. Pour most of the oil from the pan, add the spice-paste and stir-fry for 2-3 minutes. Then, add the fish sauce, tamarind water and sugar and bring to the boil. Reduce the heat and allow to simmer for 5 minutes, stirring occasionally. Finally, add the coconut milk, stir to blend thoroughly and bring back to the boil. Pour the sauce over the fish and serve.

While most Western kitchens use a food processor for pounding and blending, the mortar and pestle remain the traditional Thai method, and are still widely used, particularly in the country.

PLA GOW LAAD PRIG *(FRIED GAROUPA WITH CHILLI SAUCE)*

PLA KAPONG NUENG LAAD PRIG
(spicy steamed red snapper)

1 red snapper
1 small ripe papaya
10 dried red chillies
3 shallots
3 cloves garlic
1 stalk lemon grass
75 g (3 oz) fish fillet
600 ml (1 pint) fish stock
2 Tbsp palm sugar
2 Tbsp fish sauce
2 Tbsp tamarind water
2 Tbsp cornflour

Clean and prepare the fish and place on a steaming rack. Cut the papaya into thin strips and arrange in criss-cross fashion over the fish, then place the rack in a wok. Soak the chillies in warm water to soften. Chop the chillies, shallots, garlic, lemon grass and fish fillet, place in a mortar and pound until smooth. Pour the stock into a saucepan and bring to the boil. Add the spice-paste and stir to blend, then add the sugar, fish sauce and tamarind water and continue to stir until the sugar has completely dissolved. Pour the sauce over the fish into the wok (the surface of the liquid should be approximately 15 mm ($^1/_2$ inch) beneath the rack). Place a lid on the wok and steam the fish for 10-12 minutes, then transfer to a serving plate. Mix the cornflour with a little water, and add to the sauce. Stir to thicken, then pour the sauce over the fish.

PLA KAPONG NUENG LAAD PRIG *(SPICY STEAMED RED SNAPPER)*

PLA POW
(grilled fish)

1 sea bass, approx 675 g (1½ lbs)
1 banana leaf

Marinade:
2 cloves garlic
4 white peppercorns
2 tsp chopped coriander root
½ tsp chopped ginger
1 tsp Maggi seasoning
2 Tbsp light soya sauce

Sauce:
3 small green chillies
3 cloves garlic
6 fresh coriander leaves
salt to taste
1 tsp palm sugar
3 Tbsp fresh lime juice
75 ml (3 fl oz) clear fish stock

Clean and prepare the fish and coat evenly with the marinade, then place on the banana leaf and set aside for 15 minutes. Then, wrap the fish up tightly in the leaf and grill for 8-12 minutes on each side. Transfer to a serving plate, open the leaf and top with the prepared sauce.

To make the marinade: place the garlic, peppercorns, coriander root and ginger in a mortar, pound until smooth, then stir in the Maggi and light soya sauces until blended.

To make the sauce: chop the chillies and garlic and shred the coriander leaves. Place in a mortar, add the salt and sugar and pound until smooth, then transfer to a small saucepan. Add the lime juice and stock and bring to the boil. Stir to blend thoroughly and allow to simmer for 2-3 minutes.

PLA PAAD KHING
(sea bass with fresh ginger)

450 g (1 lb) sea bass fillets
25 mm (1 inch) knob fresh ginger
2 fresh red chillies
2 fresh green chillies
2 cloves garlic
2 spring onions
4 dried black mushrooms
75 ml (3 fl oz) vegetable oil
75 g (3 oz) preserved peas
2 Tbsp fish sauce
2 tsp sugar
freshly ground white pepper
fresh coriander leaves

Remove the skin from the fish and ensure no small bones remain, then cut into thick slices. Slice the ginger, cut the chillies into fine julienne strips, crush the garlic and cut the spring onions into 15 mm lengths. Soak the mushrooms in warm water for 40 minutes, then discard the hard stems and slice the caps. Heat the oil in a wok and sauté the ginger and garlic for 3-4 minutes, then add the fish, mushrooms and preserved peas and retain over a moderate heat, stirring occasionally, until the fish is almost cooked. Add the chillies, spring onion, fish sauce, sugar and freshly ground white pepper and stir to blend thoroughly. Continue to cook for a further 2 minutes, then transfer to a serving dish and garnish with fresh coriander leaves.

HAW MOG PLA
(spicy steamed fish with coconut)

450 g (1 lb) fish fillets
3 Tbsp red curry paste
2 Tbsp fish sauce
3 Tbsp shredded coconut
salt to taste
freshly ground black pepper
2 eggs
125 g (4 oz) cabbage
1 fresh red chilli
1 fresh green chilli
banana leaves
250 ml (9 fl oz) coconut cream

Remove the skin from the fish and ensure no small bones remain, then flake and place into a large bowl. Add the curry paste, fish sauce and shredded coconut, season to taste with salt and freshly ground black pepper and stir. Break the eggs into the bowl and continue to stir until the mixture is thoroughly blended (the mixture should be thick, but if it is too stiff, add a small quantity of coconut milk). Shred the cabbage and cut the chillies into fine julienne strips. Line a pan with the banana leaves and place a layer of shredded cabbage along the bottom. Add the fish mixture and top with thick coconut cream and strips of chilli. Cover the pan, place over boiling water and steam for 25-30 minutes, then transfer to a serving dish.

Note: If banana leaves are not available, substitute aluminium foil.

GAENG KHUA NUEA
(fish and vegetable curry)

450 g (1 lb) blackfish fillets
2 shallots
2 cloves garlic
2 fresh red chillies
2 small green chillies
4 Tbsp vegetable oil
2 tsp shrimp paste
125 g (4 oz) long green beans
1 small cauliflower
75 g (3 oz) bean sprouts
12 small mushrooms
1 tsp fish sauce
salt to taste
freshly ground white pepper
fresh coriander leaves

Grill the fish and allow to cool. Remove the skin and ensure no small bones remain. Take 125 g (4 oz) of the fish and mash with a fork, then cut the remainder into small bite-size pieces. Chop the shallots, garlic and chillies and sauté these in very hot oil for 2 minutes. Add the shrimp paste and continue to cook, stirring frequently, for a further 4 minutes, then remove from the oil and combine with the mashed fish. Cut the beans into short lengths, break the cauliflower into florets, trim the bean sprouts and halve the mushrooms. In a large saucepan, bring approximately 600 ml (1 pint) water to a rapid boil. Add the prepared spice-paste and stir well. Remove any surface scum from the water and then add the vegetables, putting in first the ones that are slowest to cook (add more water if necessary). When all the vegetables are cooked, add the fish sauce and season to taste with salt and freshly ground white pepper, then add the chunks of grilled fish and bring back to the boil. Reduce the heat and allow to simmer for a further 2 minutes, then transfer to a serving dish and garnish with fresh coriander leaves.

POULTRY & MEAT

The abundance of fish, its comparatively low market price and its favoured position in an ever-increasing health-conscious world, tend to place poultry and meat into second place in the average Thai meal. Certainly, in homes where the food budget must be carefully planned (and, surely, that applies to most of us these days), meat is served more as a 'special treat' rather than an everyday source of protein.

Generally, chickens and ducks are not cooked whole; rather, the meat is cut into bite-size pieces (usually de-boned but seldom with the skin removed), marinated and cooked with herbs, spices and vegetables. One exception to this is the very popular barbecued chicken which is served, with a variety of dips and sauces, at restaurants and roadside stalls.

The Chinese influence ensures the popularity of pork but a greater proportion of the meat dishes, certainly the curries, are based on beef. As this meat comes from the buffalo, it sometimes requires treating with a little extra 'tender loving care' but, such being second nature to the Thai cook, the succulent end results compare favourably with dishes cooked with prime American and Scottish beef.

GAENG PHED PED
(duck and vegetables)

1 duck, approx 900 g (2 lbs)
salt
freshly ground black pepper
3 Tbsp dark soya sauce
4 dried black mushrooms
400 g (14 oz) squash
2 cloves garlic
1 small onion
oil for deep frying
1.25 litres (2 pints) chicken stock
2 pickled limes
2 tsp cornflour

Clean and prepare the duck and cut into pieces (with bone). Place in a shallow dish, season with salt, freshly ground black pepper and soya sauce and allow to stand for 40 minutes. Soak the mushrooms in warm water for 40 minutes, then discard the hard stems and cut the caps in half. Peel the squash and cut into bite-size pieces and finely chop the garlic and onion. Heat the oil in a large saucepan and deep-fry the duck for 3-4 minutes, to brown and seal. Remove the duck and drain thoroughly on kitchen paper. Pour away most of the oil from the pan, then add the garlic and onion and sauté for 3-4 minutes. Replace the duck, pour in the stock and bring to the boil. Cover the pan, reduce the heat and simmer gently for approximately 90 minutes, until the duck is almost cooked. Remove the lid from the pan, add the mushrooms, squash and pickled limes and continue to cook over a moderate heat for a further 10-15 minutes until the duck is tender. Transfer the pieces of duck to a serving plate and surround with the mushroom and squash. Strain the stock, pour 400 ml (14 fl oz) into a fresh saucepan and bring back to the boil. Mix the cornflour with a small quantity of water, add this to the pan and stir to thicken before pouring the sauce over the duck.

OG GAI SOD SAI
(stuffed chicken breasts)

2 chicken breasts
2 Tbsp dark soya sauce
225 g (8 oz) lean pork
2 tinned water chestnuts
2 large fresh mushrooms
1 clove garlic
2 fresh red chillies
1 tsp chopped coriander root
1 egg
2 tsp rice flour
1/4 tsp salt
freshly ground black pepper
oil for deep frying

De-bone the chicken breasts, flatten slightly and score the skin a number of times, then rub the soya sauce into the skin and set aside for 30 minutes. Mince the pork and place in a mixing bowl. Finely chop the water chestnuts, mushrooms, garlic, chillies and coriander root and crush lightly with a wooden spoon, then add to the pork. Beat the egg and add to the mixture together with the flour, salt and freshly ground black pepper. Mix thoroughly, then spread evenly over the chicken breasts. Roll the breasts, secure with thread and place in the refrigerator for 1 hour. To cook, heat oil in a wok until it starts to smoke then reduce to a moderate heat and deep-fry the chicken until it is tender and the outside is golden and crispy, approximately 15 minutes.

GAI HAW BAI TOEY
(fried chicken in pandanus leaves)

4 chicken thighs
2 cloves garlic
1 shallot
15 mm (½ inch) knob fresh ginger
1 tsp chopped coriander root
1 tsp chopped lemon grass
6 black peppercorns
¼ tsp salt
2 Tbsp chilli sauce
2 Tbsp dark soya sauce
2 Tbsp Worcestershire sauce
125 ml (4 oz) thick coconut milk
2 tsp palm sugar
fresh pandanus leaves
oil for deep frying

De-bone the chicken, remove the skin and cut the meat into cubes. Chop the garlic, shallot and ginger and place in a mortar together with the coriander root, lemon grass, peppercorns and salt and pound into a smooth paste. Transfer the paste to a shallow dish and add the chilli sauce, soya sauce, Worcestershire sauce, coconut milk and palm sugar. Stir to blend thoroughly, then add the pieces of chicken and set aside for 40 minutes. Cut the leaves into strips 25 mm (1 inch) wide and place a piece of chicken (still coated with marinade) on top of each, then wrap securely. Heat the oil in a wok until it starts to smoke and fry the chicken until tender, approximately 10 minutes. Remove with a slotted spoon and transfer directly to a serving plate (the chicken should only be removed from the leaf just prior to eating).

GAI YAANG *(barbecued chicken)*

1 whole chicken
10 cloves garlic
15 black peppercorns
3 coriander roots
¼ tsp salt

Dip:
4 dried red chillies
2 cloves garlic
75 g (3 oz) sugar
3 Tbsp vinegar
pinch of salt

Clean and prepare the chicken and, using a sharp knife, cut along the breast bone and spread the bird open, then press lightly to flatten. Place the garlic, peppercorns, coriander roots and salt in a mortar, pound unil smooth, then spread evenly over the inside of the chicken and set aside for 1 hour. Barbecue over a moderate charcoal fire for approximately 1 hour until well cooked on both sides, then cut into small pieces and serve with the dip.

To make the dip: soak the chillies in warm water until soft, then drain and crush together with the garlic. Pour 125 ml (4 fl oz) water into a pan, add the sugar and stir over a moderate heat until the sugar has dissolved. Then, add the chilli, garlic, vinegar and salt, stir well and cook for a further minute.

PANAENG GAI *(dry chicken curry)*

4 chicken thighs
1 chicken breast
3 Tbsp light soya sauce
freshly ground black pepper
125 g (4 oz) plain flour
125 ml (4 fl oz) vegetable oil
2 Tbsp curry paste
250 ml (9 fl oz) thick coconut milk
3 Tbsp chopped roasted peanuts
2 Tbsp palm sugar
2 Tbsp fish sauce
fresh basil leaves

De-bone the chicken and cut the meat into thick slices, then season with soya sauce and black pepper and coat with the flour. Heat the oil in a wok and stir-fry the chicken until it is well browned, then remove and pour away most of the oil. Reheat the wok, then add the curry paste and cook over a moderate heat, stirring continuously. Add the coconut milk and bring to the boil. Continue to boil until the liquid has reduced by half, then add the peanuts, sugar, fish sauce and chicken and stir well. Retain over a fairly high heat until the chicken is tender and most of the liquid has been absorbed, then transfer to a serving plate and garnish with fresh basil leaves.

GAENG PED GAI
(curried chicken)

675 g (1½ lbs) chicken meat
10 dried red chillies
3 shallots
2 cloves garlic
25 mm (1 inch) knob fresh Kha
(Siamese ginger)
1 stalk lemon grass
2 tsp chopped coriander root
¼ tsp chopped mace
½ tsp chopped nutmeg
½ tsp chopped Kaffir lime peel
1 tsp roasted coriander seeds
1 tsp roasted cumin seeds
2 Tbsp shrimp paste
salt to taste
freshly ground black pepper
3 Tbsp vegetable oil
125 g (4 oz) bamboo shoots
600 ml (1 pint) thick coconut milk
fresh coriander leaves

Remove the skin and cut the chicken meat into small pieces. Soak the chillies in warm water to soften. Chop the chillies, shallots, garlic, ginger and lemon grass and place in a mortar, together with the coriander root, mace, nutmeg, lime peel, coriander seeds, cumin seeds, shrimp paste, salt and pepper, then pound until smooth. Heat the oil in a wok and stir-fry the spice-paste for 4-5 minutes, then add the chicken meat and cook for a further minute. Cut the bamboo shoot into fine shreds and add to the pan. Pour in the coconut milk, stir to blend thoroughly and bring slowly to the boil. Continue to cook over a moderate heat until the chicken is tender, then transfer to a serving dish and garnish with fresh coriander leaves.

GAENG PED GAI *(CURRIED CHICKEN)*

TOM KEM GAI
(chicken casserole)

8 chicken legs
2 Tbsp rice flour
4 dried black mushrooms
2 shallots
1 clove garlic
15 mm (½ inch) knob fresh ginger
½ tsp chopped coriander root
salt to taste
freshly ground black pepper
3 Tbsp vegetable oil
3 Tbsp brown sugar
2 Tbsp light soya sauce
4 hard-boiled eggs
fresh coriander leaves

Dust the chicken legs with flour. Soak the mushrooms in warm water for 40 minutes and discard the hard stems. Chop the shallots, garlic and ginger and pound together with the coriander root, salt and freshly ground black pepper. Heat the oil in a large casserole dish and cook the spice-paste for 5 minutes to give flavour to the oil. Then, discard the spice-paste leaving only the oil. Add the sugar and cook over a low heat, stirring continuously, until the mixture becomes syrupy. Add the soya sauce together with 250 ml (9fl oz) cold water and bring to the boil. Add the chicken legs and the mushrooms and place a cover on the dish. Reduce the heat and simmer for 45 minutes, then add the hard-boiled eggs and continue to cook slowly for a further 30 minutes. Garnish with fresh coriander leaves and serve.

Garlands of colourful fragrant flowers are used as decorations on many occasions in Thailand.

TOM KEM GAI *(CHICKEN CASSEROLE)*

MOO WAAN
(glazed pork)

450 g (1 lb) streaky bacon
2 cloves garlic
2 Tbsp vegetable oil
2 Tbsp light soya sauce
2 Tbsp fish sauce
100 g (4 oz) palm sugar

Cut the pork into bite-size pieces and chop the garlic finely. Heat the oil in a wok, add the garlic and stir for 2 minutes, then add the pork and continue to cook, stirring frequently, for approximately 5 minutes until golden brown. Add the soya sauce, fish sauce and sugar and stir to blend, then add 75 ml (3 fl oz) water and bring to the boil. Reduce the heat and simmer until the sauce becomes syrupy, then remove with a slotted spoon and transfer to a serving plate.

Note: While this can be served as part of a meal, it also makes a delicious snack served with an icy cold glass of Thai beer.

MOO GROB
(crispy fried pork)

325 g (12 oz) pork belly
1 tsp salt
oil for deep frying
2 shallots
2 cloves garlic
25 mm (1 inch) knob fresh ginger
3 small tomatoes
2 fresh red chillies
2 fresh green chillies
1 tsp chopped coriander root
2 Tbsp dark soya sauce
2 Tbsp rice wine
3 Tbsp chicken stock
freshly ground black pepper
2 tsp fish sauce

With a sharp knife, score the pork skin, approximately every 15 mm (1/2 inch) and rub in salt. Set aside for 30 minutes, then cut into strips. Heat the oil until it begins to smoke and deep-fry the pork until the skin is golden and crispy. Remove the pork, drain on kitchen paper, pat dry and allow to cool, then cut into small dice. Chop the shallots, garlic, ginger and tomatoes. Finely chop 1 red and 1 green chilli and cut the remaining 2 into fine julienne strips. Pour a small quantity of oil into a wok and sauté the shallot, garlic and ginger for 3-4 minutes. Then, add the chopped chilli, tomato, coriander root, soya sauce, wine and stock and bring to the boil. Add the pork, season with freshly ground black pepper and stir to blend thoroughly. Allow to simmer for 15 minutes, then add the fish sauce, stir again and cook for a further 3-4 minutes. Transfer to a serving plate and garnish with the julienne strips of chilli. Serve with a sweet plum sauce dip.

GAENG MOO TEPO
(pork curry with water spinach)

450 g (1 lb) pork
450 g (1 lb) spinach
6 dried red chillies
4 shallots
4 cloves garlic
25 mm (1 inch) knob fresh Kha
(Siamese ginger)
3 stalks lemon grass
1 tsp chopped coriander root
1 tsp chopped Kaffir lime peel
½ tsp cumin seeds
1 tsp shrimp paste
salt to taste
600 ml (1 pint) thick coconut milk
2 Tbsp fish sauce

Slice the pork into small pieces. Wash the spinach under running water and remove the hard stems. Soak the chillies in warm water to soften. Chop the chillies, shallots, garlic, ginger and lemon grass and place in a mortar, together with the coriander root, lime peel, cumin seeds, shrimp paste and salt, then pound until smooth. Pour 150 ml (5 fl oz) coconut milk into a wok and bring to the boil, then add the spice-paste and stir-fry until it gives off a fragrant aroma. Add the pork and remaining coconut milk and bring back to the boil. Reduce the heat and allow to simmer slowly for 10 minutes, then add the spinach, season with fish sauce and cook for a further minute.

MOO SARONG
(pork balls wrapped in noodles)

450 g (1 lb) lean pork
4 tinned water chestnuts
5 fresh mushrooms
3 shallots
4 coriander roots
3 cloves garlic
6 black peppercorns
½ tsp salt
1 egg, lightly whisked
2 Tbsp plain flour
2 salted egg yolks
rice vermicelli noodles

Mince the pork, water chestnuts, mushrooms and shallots and place in a mixing bowl. Chop the coriander root and garlic and place in a mortar together with the peppercorns and salt, then pound until smooth. Add the spice-paste to the pork mixture, together with the whisked egg and flour. Blend thoroughly and make into small balls approximately 25 mm (1 inch) in diameter, encasing a tiny piece of salted egg yolk in the centre of each. Soak the noodles in warm water until soft and drain off all the water, then sprinkle a small amount of cooking oil on the noodles and toss well to prevent them from sticking together. Wrap sufficient noodles around each pork ball to cover completely. Heat the remaining oil in a large wok and cook until the pork balls are golden and crispy. Serve with small bowls of light soya sauce, Tabasco and plum sauce for dipping.

PAAD LOOG CHIN
(deep-fried pork balls with vegetables)

575 g (1¼ lb) pork
2 dried black mushrooms
2 shallots
2 tinned water chestnuts
75 g (3 oz) bamboo shoots
1 clove garlic
½ tsp chopped coriander root
2 tsp fresh lime juice
1 tsp sugar
salt to taste
freshly ground black pepper
1 lightly whisked egg
2 Tbsp plain flour
oil for deep frying

Trim excess fat from the pork and pass the meat through a mincer. Soak the mushrooms in warm water for 40 minutes, then discard the hard stems. Finely chop the mushroom caps, shallots, water chestnuts and bamboo shoots. Chop the garlic finely and place in a mortar, together with the coriander root, lime juice, sugar, salt and pepper and pound until smooth. Place the spice-paste into a mixing bowl, add the pork and egg, stir to blend thoroughly and set aside for 30 minutes. Then, add the flour and finely chopped vegetables, mix well and shape into small balls, approximately 25 mm (1 inch) in diameter. Heat the oil in a wok until it is very hot, reduce to a moderate heat and deep-fry the meat-balls for 6-10 minutes. Then, remove from the oil with a slotted spoon and serve on top of freshly cooked vegetables.

PAAD LOOG CHIN *(DEEP-FRIED PORK BALLS WITH VEGETABLES)*

GAENG GARI NUEA
(beef curry)

450 g (1 lb) rump steak
175 g (6 oz) eggplant
8 dried red chillies
2 shallots
2 cloves garlic
15 mm (½ inch) knob fresh ginger
15 mm (½ inch) knob fresh Kha
(Siamese ginger)
2 stalks lemon grass
6 black peppercorns
1 tsp chopped Kaffir lime peel
½ tsp cumin seeds
½ tsp coriander seeds
100 ml (4 fl oz) coconut oil
550 ml (18 fl oz) thick coconut milk
¼ tsp dried basil
550 ml (18 fl oz) thin coconut milk
2 Tbsp fish sauce
fresh basil leaves
freshly shredded red chilli

Slice the beef and chop the eggplant into bite-size pieces. Soak the chillies in warm water until soft, drain and then pat dry. Chop the chillies, shallots, garlic, ginger and lemon grass and place in a mortar. Pound lightly, then add the peppercorns, lime peel, cumin and coriander seeds and continue to pound until smooth. Heat the oil in a wok until moderately hot and stir-fry the spice-paste for 4-5 minutes, then add the thick coconut milk and continue to stir until the liquid has reduced by half. Then, add the beef, eggplant, dried basil and half the thin coconut milk and bring almost to the boil. Allow to simmer until the beef is cooked, then add the fish sauce and stir in the remaining milk. Bring to a rapid boil and allow the liquid to reduce slightly, then transfer to a serving bowl and garnish with fresh basil leaves and shreds of red chilli.

GAENG GARI NUEA *(BEEF CURRY)*

GAENG HAANG LAE
(curried meats, northern style)

225 g (8 oz) lean pork
225 g (8 oz) lean beef
5 dried red chillies
4 shallots
4 cloves garlic
2 tsp red curry paste
1 tsp shrimp paste
1/2 tsp turmeric powder
salt to taste
3 Tbsp vegetable oil
3 Tbsp tamarind water
1 tsp fresh lime juice
2 Tbsp fish sauce
2 Tbsp palm sugar
freshly shredded red chillies

Cut the pork and beef into bite-size pieces. Bring 600 ml (1 pint) water to the boil, add the meat and cook until tender. Remove the meat, bring the water to a rapid boil and reduce by half. Meanwhile, soak the chillies in warm water to soften. Chop the chillies, shallots and garlic and place in a mortar, together with the curry paste, shrimp paste, turmeric and salt, and pound until smooth. Heat the oil in a wok, add the spice-paste and stir-fry until it gives off a fragrant aroma. Then, add the meat and cooking stock, stir well and bring back to the boil. Add the tamarind water, lime juice, fish sauce and sugar and stir to blend thoroughly. Transfer to a serving dish and garnish with fresh red chillies.

NUEA PAAD PRIG
(sautéed beef with chillies)

450 g (1 lb) rump steak
1/2 tsp salt
freshly ground black pepper
3 dried black mushrooms
1 large onion
1 clove garlic
4 fresh red chillies
3 Tbsp vegetable oil
100 ml (4 fl oz) beef stock
2 Tbsp light soya sauce
2 tsp oyster sauce
2 tsp rice wine

Cut the beef into bite-size pieces and season with salt and freshly ground black pepper. Soak the mushrooms in warm water for 40 minutes, discard the hard stems and slice the caps. Chop the onion and garlic and cut the chillies into fine julienne strips. Heat the oil in a wok and sauté the onion and garlic for 3-4 minutes, then add the beef and chillies and continue to cook for a further 2 minutes, stirring frequently. Pour in the stock and bring to the boil. Add the mushrooms, soya sauce, oyster sauce and wine and adjust seasonings to taste. Reduce the heat and continue to cook over a moderate heat until the beef is tender.

PANAENG NUEA
(chilli beef)

450 g (1 lb) rump steak
1/4 tsp salt
freshly ground white pepper
8 dried red chillies
25 mm (1 inch) knob fresh Kha
(Siamese ginger)
3 shallots
2 stalks lemon grass
6 cloves garlic
1/2 tsp coriander root
2 tsp chopped Kaffir lime peel
10 black peppercorns
1 tsp shrimp paste
900 ml (1 1/2 pints) thin coconut milk
400 ml (14 fl oz) coconut cream
175 g (6 oz) crushed roasted peanuts
12 fresh basil leaves
2 Tbsp fish sauce
2 Tbsp palm sugar
shredded Kaffir lime leaves
freshly shredded red chillies

Cut the beef into thin slices and season with salt and freshly ground white pepper. Soak the chillies in warm water to soften. Chop the chillies, ginger, shallots, lemon grass and garlic and place in a mortar together with the coriander root, lime peel, peppercorns and shrimp paste, then pound until smooth. Pour the coconut milk into a wok and bring to the boil. Add the beef and cook until tender, then remove, set aside and discard the milk. Pour the coconut cream into the wok and bring to the boil. Reduce the heat and simmer until the oil floats to the surface, then add the spice-paste and cook for 4-5 minutes, stirring continuously. Add the beef, crushed roasted peanuts, 8 basil leaves, fish sauce and sugar, then stir well and cook slowly for a further 2 minutes. Finally, transfer to a serving dish and garnish with remaining basil leaves, lime leaves and chillies.

KHIAW WAAN NUEA
(green curry with beef)

450 g (1 lb) topside
1/2 tsp salt
1/4 tsp freshly ground white pepper
4 Tbsp vegetable oil
3 Tbsp green curry paste
750 ml (1 1/4 pints) thick coconut milk
2 tsp sugar
1 tsp fish sauce
2 Tbsp light soya sauce
2 fresh green chillies
freshly chopped sweet basil leaves
freshly chopped coriander leaves
freshly chopped lime leaves

Cut the beef into thin slices and season with salt and freshly ground white pepper. Heat the oil in a wok, add the curry paste and stir over a moderate heat for 4-5 minutes, then add the beef and continue to stir-fry for a further 2-3 minutes, until the meat starts to change colour. Next, add the coconut milk and bring to the boil, stirring continuously. Then, reduce the heat, add the sugar, fish sauce and soya sauce and allow to simmer for 30-40 minutes. Remove the seeds from the chillies, chop finely and add to the curry together with the freshly chopped leaves. Stir well and continue to cook slowly for a further 10 minutes before serving.

RICE & NOODLES

For good reason Thailand is affectionately known as the "rice bowl of Asia" for it is, indeed, one of the world's greatest rice-growing countries and exports far beyond the boundaries of Asia.

As the grain is as important to the economy as it is to the diet, it is treated with a respect bordering on reverence and numerous ritual ceremonies, associated with the planting and harvesting, are celebrated throughout the year.

The long-grain white variety is the most commonly used and is generally steamed to a light and fluffy texture to provide the ubiquitous bowl of rice served at humble family meals and formal banquets alike. Glutinous rice (paradoxically gluten-free but which becomes sweet and sticky when cooked) is very popular in the north of the country and is widely used in making desserts.

Rice flour, milled from both the polished white and brown grains, is used in making different styles of noodles which, when fried together with other ingredients or used in soups, provide nutritious and satisfying single-dish meals, most often enjoyed at roadside stalls.

KHAO PAAD SUPPAROD
(fried rice in pineapple)

300 g (10 oz) long-grain rice
1 large pineapple
125 g (4 oz) fresh prawns
125 g (4 oz) crabmeat
125 g (4 oz) Chinese sausage
1 shallot
2 cloves garlic
2 fresh red chillies
4 Tbsp vegetable oil
2 tsp fish sauce
freshly ground black pepper
2 Tbsp light soya sauce
2 Tbsp crispy-fried shallots

First, boil the rice until it is three-quarters cooked, then drain and set aside. Cut the pineapple in half lengthways. Cut out the flesh, reserving half for another occasion, and cut the remainder into small cubes. Shell and de-vein the prawns and chop into small pieces. Shred the crabmeat and chop the sausage. Finely chop the shallot, garlic and chillies. Heat the oil in a wok, add the shallot, garlic and chillies and sauté for 3-4 minutes. Add the prawns and continue to cook for a further 3 minutes, then add the crabmeat and sausage and stir to blend thoroughly. Add the rice and season with fish sauce, soya sauce and freshly ground black pepper and, if necessary, add a little more oil. Stir well and cook over a fairly high heat for approximately 3 minutes until the rice is fluffy and fully cooked. Stir in half the diced pineapple and cook for a further minute. To serve fill the pineapple shells with the rice and sprinkle crispy fried shallot on top and garnish with the remaining pineapple.

KHAO PAAD NAAM PRIG THOD
(spicy fried rice with prawns)

300 g (10 oz) long-grain rice
225 g (8 oz) fresh prawns
4 Tbsp vegetable oil
3 Tbsp shrimp paste dip
tomato wedges
cucumber wedges

Shrimp Paste Dip:
3 cloves garlic
3 small green chillies
2 Tbsp shrimp paste
3 Tbsp fresh lime juice
3 Tbsp fish sauce

Steam the rice until fully cooked and keep warm. Shell and de-vein the prawns, leaving the tails intact. Heat the oil in a wok and fry the prawns for approximately 3 minutes until they turn pink and curl. Remove and drain on kitchen paper. Place the shrimp paste dip in the same wok and stir until fragrant, then add the rice, mix well and stir fry for 2 minutes. Transfer to a serving plate, arrange the fried prawns on top and garnish with the tomato and cucumber.

To make the dip: chop the garlic and chillies and place in a mortar together with the shrimp paste and pound until smooth, then add the lime juice and fish sauce and stir until blended.

Note: Any remaining dip can be frozen and kept for a fairly lengthy period, until required.

MEE GROB
(crispy fried noodles)

450 g (1 lb) rice vermicelli noodles
oil for deep frying
1 chicken breast
125 g (4 oz) lean pork
2 shallots
4 cloves garlic
3 Tbsp crispy-fried yellow bean curd
75 g (3 oz) bean sprouts
salt to taste
freshly ground black pepper
5 eggs
3 Tbsp vinegar
3 Tbsp fish sauce
4 Tbsp sugar
½ tsp roasted chilli powder
fresh coriander leaves

Sprinkle the noodles with cold water and set aside to soften. Heat the oil in a wok until very hot, add the noodles and cook over a high heat until crisp and golden. Remove from the oil, drain and wrap in a paper towel, so they remain crisp, and keep warm until needed. Pour off all but 4 Tbsp of oil from the wok. De-bone and slice the chicken breast and dice the pork. Finely chop the shallots and garlic. Replace the wok over a moderate heat and sauté the shallot and garlic until crisp and golden. Then, add the chicken and pork and stir-fry for 5 minutes. If necessary, add a little more oil, then add the bean curd and bean sprouts and season to taste with salt and pepper. Lightly whisk the eggs and stir in a little at a time, cooking until the eggs are set. Sprinkle on the vinegar, fish sauce and sugar and stir until the liquid has evaporated. Finally, add the roasted chilli powder, reduce to a low heat, then add the noodles. Toss to mix and continue cooking a further minute. Transfer to a serving dish and garnish with fresh coriander leaves.

GUAY TIAW PAAD THAI
(stir-fried noodle, Thai style)

350 g (12 oz) flat rice noodles
175 g (6 oz) fresh prawns
125 g (4 oz) roasted pork
75 g (3 oz) bean sprouts
2 fresh red chillies
2 shallots
3 Tbsp fish sauce
2 Tbsp sugar
2 Tbsp tamarind water
1 tsp lime juice
4 Tbsp vegetable oil
2 Tbsp light soya sauce
freshly ground black pepper
shredded red chilli

Cut the noodles into strips about 50 mm (2 inches) wide. (If using dried noodles, already cut, use only 225 g (8 oz) and soak in warm water until soft.) Shell and de-vein the prawns, then cut in half lengthways. Shred the pork and trim the bean sprouts. Place the chillies, shallots, fish sauce and sugar in a mortar and pound, then add the tamarind water and lime juice, mix well, and continue to pound until smooth. Heat the oil in a wok until very hot, then add the spice-paste and stir-fry until there is a fragrant aroma. Add the shrimps and stir to ensure they are evenly coated with the paste. Then add the noodles, season with soya sauce and freshly ground black pepper and, if necessary, add a little water. Stir-fry for 2-3 minutes, then add the pork and bean sprouts and toss until well mixed. Continue cooking for a further 2 minutes, then transfer to a serving dish and garnish with shredded red chilli.

SALADS & VEGETABLES

Unlike the generally uninspiring 'side-dishes' of Western cuisines, Thai salads are a significant part of most meals and, indeed, when slices of meat and various seafoods are included, they may well be served as a main course.

To the Thai cook who takes such pride in presenting meals that are as appealing to look at as they are to eat, the preparation of a salad offers the very best opportunity of achieving these dual objectives. Certainly, the sight of a colourful, multi-textured plate of freshly-picked vegetables, aromatic herbs, flavourful leaves and exotic fruits – all chopped, sliced, spiced, blended and topped with a choice of crushed roasted peanuts, crispy fried shallot and garlic, various shredded leaves and strips of red and green chilli – should excite the gastronomic juices of even the most blasé international gourmet.

Vegetables are often included in soups or cooked together with fish, poultry or meat but are less frequently served as a dish apart. They may be stir-fried, steamed or boiled but the cooking time is always minimal in order that flavour, texture and 'original goodness' are all retained.

YAAM YAI
(mixed vegetable salad)

1 small head of lettuce
½ small cucumber
1 tomato
1 small green papaya
2 spring onions
100 g (4 oz) cooked shrimps
75 g (3 oz) cooked pork
75 g (3 oz) cooked pork liver
1 hard-boiled egg, quartered

Dressing:
2 Tbsp roasted peanuts
2 fresh red chillies
4 Tbsp fresh lime juice
3 Tbsp fish sauce
2 tsp sugar

Core the lettuce, wash the leaves and arrange in a large salad bowl. Slice the cucumber, tomato and papaya and lightly crush the spring onions, then place all in a mixing bowl. Shell and de-vein the shrimps. Slice the liver and pork and add to the bowl, together with the shrimps. Pour in the prepared dressing, toss to mix thoroughly and transfer to the salad bowl and garnish with the quartered egg.

To make the dressing: crush the peanuts and mince the chillies, then mix together with the lime juice, fish sauce and sugar. Stir until the sugar has dissolved.

YAAM POLAMAI
(Thai herbed fruit salad)

1 orange
1 apple
125 ml (4 fl oz) fresh lime juice
125 g (4 oz) grapes
125 g (4 oz) pitted lychees
8 tinned water chestnuts
125 g (4 oz) cooked prawns
75 g (3 oz) cooked chicken meat
salt to taste
2 tsp sugar
3 Tbsp crispy-fried garlic
3 Tbsp crispy-fried shallots
3 Tbsp crushed roasted peanuts
shredded red chillies
shredded coriander leaves

Peel and chop the orange and peel, core and dice the apple. Sprinkle a small quantity of lime juice over the apple to prevent discolouration. Halve and pit the grapes and slice the lychees and water chestnuts. Slice the prawns and shred the chicken meat. Mix the salt and sugar with the remaining lime juice and stir until the sugar has dissolved, then add the prawn and chicken and mix well. Add the fruits and chestnuts and half the garlic, shallot and peanuts, then toss gently to mix, taking care not to damage the texture of the fruit. To serve: place the salad in hollow orange halves, sprinkle the remaining garlic, shallot and peanuts on top and garnish with the shredded chillies and coriander.

A tasty custard steamed in a carved pumpkin is just one example of how the Thai cook manages to please the eye as well as the palate.

YAAM SOM-O (pomelo salad)

1 ripe pomelo
150 g (5 oz) cooked shrimps
75 g (3 oz) roasted pork
2 Tbsp fresh lime juice
2 Tbsp fish sauce
2 Tbsp chilli jam
2 Tbsp palm sugar
2 Tbsp roasted grated coconut
175 ml (6 fl oz) coconut cream
sweet basil leaves

Peel the pomelo and shred the flesh. Shell and de-vein the shrimps. Mince half the shrimps and chop the pork. Place the lime juice, fish sauce, chilli jam and sugar in a bowl and stir to mix. Then, add the minced shrimp, pork, grated coconut and coconut cream and continue stirring until blended. Add the fruit and toss to coat thoroughly. Transfer to a serving plate, arrange the remaining shrimps around the side and garnish with sweet basil leaves.

YAAM THUA POO
(winged bean salad)

150 g (5 oz) winged beans
3 shallots
125 g (4 oz) cooked shrimps
75 g (3 oz) cooked chicken meat
3 small green chillies
1 fresh red chilli
75 g (3 oz) roasted peanuts
75 ml (3 oz) coconut cream
2 Tbsp fish sauce
3 Tbsp fresh lime juice
2 Tbsp sugar
2 Tbsp chilli sauce
2 Tbsp roasted grated coconut

Slice the winged beans crossways and blanch in rapidly boiling water. Remove and drain and plunge into iced water in order to retain colour and crispy texture. Slice the shallots, halve the shrimps and shred the chicken. Crush the chillies and roasted peanuts and place in a mixing bowl. Add the shrimps and chicken together with the coconut cream, fish sauce, lime juice, sugar and chilli sauce. Stir to mix, then add the winged beans and shallots and toss to mix. Transfer to a serving bowl and sprinkle the grated coconut on top.

YAAM NUEA (Thai beef salad)

450 g (1 lb) beef fillet
2 cloves garlic
6 fresh coriander leaves
3 Tbsp sugar
3 tsp light soya sauce
2 tsp fresh lime juice
salt to taste
freshly ground black pepper
2 spring onions
6 fresh red chillies
2 Tbsp vegetable oil
lettuce leaves

Cook the beef to medium rare, or as preferred, and cut into small thin slices. Crush the garlic and finely chop 2 of the coriander leaves and place in a mortar, together with the sugar, soya sauce, lime juice, salt and freshly ground black pepper, then pound until smooth. Cut the spring onions and chillies into very thin slices. Heat the oil in a wok and stir-fry the spice-paste for 3-4 minutes, then add the beef and cook for a further minute. Remove the beef and allow to cool. To serve: place the lettuce leaves on a plate and add the beef. Then, sprinkle the spring onion and chilli on top and garnish with the remaining coriander leaves.

YAAM NUEA *(THAI BEEF SALAD)*

GOONG YAAM
(spiced prawn salad)

400 g (14 oz) cooked prawns
10 fresh mint leaves
1 shallot
15 mm (1/2 inch) knob fresh ginger
2 fresh red chillies
1 stalk lemon grass
1 clove garlic
2 tsp palm sugar
2 tsp fish sauce
4 Tbsp fresh lime juice
freshly ground black pepper
lettuce leaves

Shell and de-vein the prawns and cut in half lengthways. Rub the inside of a salad bowl with half the mint leaves. Finely chop the shallot, ginger, chillies and lemon grass and crush the garlic, then place in the bowl, together with the sausage, fish sauce and lime juice. Stir to blend thoroughly, then add the prawns, season to taste with freshly ground black pepper and toss well. Transfer to a fresh bowl, lined with luttuce leaves and garnish with the remaining mint leaves.

MIANG PLA TOO
(spicy mackerel salad)

4 small mackerel
100 g (4 fl oz) vegetable oil
4 shallots
25 mm (1 inch) knob fresh ginger
4 fresh red chillies
4 small green chillies
75 g (3 oz) roasted peanuts
1/2 small green mango
3 Tbsp fresh lime juice
1 tsp shredded lime peel
salt to taste
freshly ground black pepper
lettuce leaves
coriander leaves

Clean and prepare the fish and steam until partially cooked. Then, heat the vegetable oil in a shallow pan and fry the fish for 4-5 minutes, turning once. Carefully remove the skin and all the bones from the fish and flake the meat, then place in a large mixing bowl. Slice the shallots and ginger and chop the chillies finely. Crush the peanuts lightly with the back of a spoon and cut the green mango into very fine shreds. Add all these ingredients to the fish, together with the lime juice, lime peel and salt and pepper to taste. Using salad servers, toss to combine thoroughly. To serve: arrange the lettuce leaves in a salad bowl, add the spicy fish and garnish with the coriander leaves.

The watermelon, with its skin of rich green and bright red flesh, makes an ideal subject for the fruit carver's skills.

MIANG PLA TOO *(SPICY MACKEREL SALAD)*

PAAG TOM GATHI
(vegetables boiled in coconut milk)

125 g (4 oz) bamboo shoots
125 g (4 oz) string beans
125 g (4 oz) baby corn
75 g (3 oz) winged beans
75 g (3 oz) shredded white cabbage
75 g (3 oz) spinach
600 ml (1 pint) thin coconut milk
salt to taste
freshly ground black pepper
4 Tbsp coconut cream

Wash and prepare all the vegetables. Pour the coconut milk into a large saucepan, add the salt and bring to the boil. Add the bamboo shoots and cook for 2 minutes, then add the string beans and winged beans and continue to cook for a further minute. Finally, add the remaining vegetables and cook for 2 minutes, then remove, drain thoroughly and arrange on a serving plate. Spoon the coconut cream on top of the vegetables and season with freshly ground black pepper.

PAAD KHAO PODE ONN GUB GAI
(baby corn with chicken)

400 g (14 oz) baby corn
3 cloves garlic
1 shallot
4 spring onions
175 g (6 oz) white chicken meat
2 Tbsp vegetable oil
salt to taste
freshly ground black pepper
2 tsp sugar
100 ml (4 fl oz) chicken stock
2 tsp cornflour

Trim the corn, wash under cold running water and drain thoroughly. Finely chop the garlic, shallot and spring onions and cut the chicken meat into thin slices. Heat the oil in a wok until it is very hot, add the garlic and shallot and sauté for 4-5 minutes until golden and crispy. Reduce the heat and add the chicken meat, salt, freshly ground black pepper and sugar and stir-fry for 2 minutes to blend well, then add the spring onion and pour in the stock. Bring to the boil, reduce the heat and simmer gently for 6 minutes, then add the corn and continue to cook a further 3 minutes. Mix the cornflour with a small quantity of cold water, add to the pan and stir to thicken slightly before serving.

PAAG BOONG PAAD
(stir-fried spinach)

450 g (1 lb) spinach
2 cloves garlic
2 Tbsp preserved soya beans
3 Tbsp vegetable oil
freshly ground black pepper
finely sliced red chilli

Remove the hard stems, then place the spinach in a colander and wash under cold running water for several minutes. Allow to drain thoroughly. Crush the garlic and mash the soya bean. Heat the oil in a wok and sauté the garlic and soya bean for 3-4 minutes, then add the spinach and cook for a further 2-3 minutes, stirring frequently. Season to taste with freshly ground black pepper, then transfer to a serving dish and garnish with finely sliced chilli.

THUA NGOK PAAD TAO HOO
(stir-fried bean sprouts and bean curd)

200 g (7 oz) bean sprouts
100 g (4 oz) bean curd
2 cloves garlic
3 spring onions
3 Tbsp vegetable oil
4 Tbsp oyster sauce
freshly ground black pepper

Trim the bean sprouts and chop the bean curd. Crush the garlic and cut the spring onions into 25 mm (1 inch) lengths. Heat the oil in a wok and sauté the garlic until it starts to brown, then add the bean sprouts, bean curd and oyster sauce and cook for 2-3 minutes, stirring frequently. Finally, stir in the spring onion and season to taste with freshly ground black pepper, then transfer to a serving dish.

PAAD PAAG NAAM MUN HOY
(broccoli in oyster sauce)

350 g (12 oz) broccoli
2 cloves garlic
2 Tbsp vegetable oil
4 Tbsp oyster sauce
2 tsp light soya sauce
freshly ground black pepper

Break the broccoli into florets and discard the tough stems. Place in a steamer over rapidly boiling water and cook for 3-4 minutes, until tender. Crush the garlic. Heat the oil in a wok and sauté the garlic until golden and crispy, then add the broccoli and oyster sauce and stir-fry for 2-3 minutes. Season to taste with salt and freshly ground black pepper, then transfer to a serving dish.

DESSERTS

Thais, unlike many of their Asian neighbours, consider a sweet course an essential and harmonious way of rounding off a well-balanced meal and much effort is made to prepare dishes pleasing both to the palate and the eye.

Not surprisingly, advantage is taken of the abundance of locally grown fruits, such as mangosteen, rambutan, jack fruit, pineapple, banana, custard apple, watermelon and mango to create delicious and colourful desserts; often to be served with bountiful amounts of fresh coconut cream or, perhaps, with coconut-flavoured custard or ice-cream.

The fruits are also used, on more formal occasions, as table decorations and, when carved in intricate designs (an art which appears deceptively simple when performed by an expert), never fail to amaze and delight first-time visitors to Thailand.

Apart from the lighter desserts, it is also customary, at the very end of a meal, to serve small 'baskets' (woven from pandanus or banana leaves), filled with sweets or 'small cakes' made from mung beans, yams, glutinous rice, coconut flesh and agar agar; often flavoured with fresh fruits and sweetened with coconut cream and palm sugar.

WOON WAAN
(sweet agar agar moulds)

2 Tbsp agar agar
200 g (7 oz) sugar
food colouring
thick coconut cream

Pour 150 ml (5 fl oz) hot water into a mixing bowl, sprinkle in the agar agar and the sugar and stir until dissolved. Add a further 600 ml (1 pint) water and stir briskly, then divide the mixture into four bowls and add a few drops of different food colouring into each. Pour into small moulds and allow to cool slightly, then refrigerate until completely set. Serve with thick coconut cream.

AI-TIM GATHI
(coconut ice-cream)

125 ml (5 fl oz) coconut water
2 Tbsp gelatine
900 ml (1½ pint) coconut cream
150 g (5 oz) granulated sugar
pinch of salt
150 g (5 oz) fresh grated coconut
2 Tbsp roasted grated coconut

Warm the coconut water in a small saucepan, and pour into a mixing bowl, sprinkle on the gelatine and stir until completely dissolved, then set aside to cool. Add the coconut cream, sugar, salt and grated coconut and blend thoroughly. Pour the mixture into a deep dish and place in the freezer. Allow to partially set, then remove and stir briskly. Replace in the freezer and repeat the stirring process three more times at approximately 20 minute intervals. Finally, allow to firmly set and top with roasted grated coconut.

TUB TIM GROB
(water chestnuts in coconut syrup)

150 g (5 oz) tinned water chestnuts
125 ml (4 fl oz) thin coconut milk
4 Tbsp sugar-syrup
pinch of salt

Finely chop the water chestnuts and place in a serving dish. Add the coconut milk, syrup, salt and a small quantity of shaved ice. Stir to blend thoroughly and serve immediately.

MED-KANOON
(mock jack fruit seeds)

200 g (7 oz) dry white lentils
125 g (4 oz) grated coconut
¼ tsp salt
450 g (1 lb) granulated sugar
5 egg yolks
few drops jasmine oil
fresh mint leaves
jasmine flowers

Soak the lentils for at least 12 hours, then cook in a steamer until soft and mash with a fork. Allow the mashed lentils to cool, then combine with the grated coconut, salt and 150 g (5 fl oz) of the sugar. Blend thoroughly, then mould the mixture into the shape of grapes and set to one side. Lightly whisk the egg yolks in a mixing bowl. Pour 350 ml (12 fl oz) water into a saucepan, add the remaining sugar and the jasmine oil and bring to the boil, stirring until the sugar has completely dissolved. Reduce the heat and retain the syrup at simmering point. Dip the lentil 'grapes' into the egg yolk to coat thoroughly, then cook in the syrup for 5 minutes. Remove to a wire rack and allow to cool. Refrigerate for at least 30 minutes, place on a serving plate and decorate with fresh mint leaves and jasmine flowers.

MED MAENG LUG NAAM GATHI
(sweet basil seeds in coconut milk)

2 Tbsp sweet basil seeds
1 green coconut
400 ml (14 fl oz) coconut cream
100 g (4 oz) palm sugar

Cover the basil seeds with cold water and leave for 20 minutes, stirring occasionally. Then remove the seeds from the water, drain well and place in a serving bowl. Open the coconut with a cleaver and discard the water. Remove the soft flesh with a small spoon and add this to the basil seeds. Warm the coconut cream in a saucepan, add the palm sugar and stir to completely dissolve. Allow the cream to cool, then pour into the bowl and stir well to mix. Chill for 1 hour before serving.

KHAO NIEW MAMUANG
(sticky rice and mango)

125 g (4 oz) glutinous rice
175 ml (6 fl oz) thick coconut milk
3 Tbsp sugar-syrup
pinch of salt
2 ripe mangoes

Soak the rice for at least 12 hours, then cook in a steamer and allow to cool. Combine the coconut milk, syrup and salt. Peel the mangoes and cut the flesh into small chunks. To serve: spoon a little rice into the bottom of individual serving dishes, add the mango and pour the coconut milk mixture on top.

FUG THONG SUNG-KHAYA
(custard in pumpkin)

1 small pumpkin
5 eggs
75 g (3 oz) palm sugar
pinch of salt
250 ml (8 fl oz) coconut cream

Cut a slice off the top of the pumpkin, remove the seeds and most of the soft pulp. In a mixing bowl, lightly whisk the eggs, add the sugar, salt and coconut cream and stir until blended. Pour the mixture into the pumpkin, replace the top of the pumpkin and cook in a steamer until the custard is set, approximately 20 minutes.

KHAO NIAW PIAG
(sticky rice and sweet corn pudding)

250 g (8 oz) glutinous rice
75 g (3 oz) granulated sugar
125 g (4 oz) tinned sweet corn
pinch of salt
sweet basil leaves

Soak the rice for at least 12 hours. Boil the rice until tender and fluffy, then remove from the heat and stir in the sugar and sweetcorn. Blend thoroughly and spoon into individual serving bowls. Season the coconut cream with salt, pour over the rice and garnish with sweet basil leaves.

LOOG CHOOB
(mock marzipan sweets)

225 g (7 oz) soya beans
225 g (7 oz) granulated sugar
125 g (4 oz) grated coconut
250 ml (8 fl oz) thick coconut milk
2 Tbsp gelatine
food colourings

Steam the soya beans until soft, then mash and place in a saucepan. Place over a moderate heat, add the sugar, grated coconut and coconut milk and stir until the mixture becomes very thick. Then, remove and allow to cool before placing in the refrigerator for 1 hour. In a bowl dissolve the gelatine in a small quantity of warm water. Mould the soya bean mixture into small shapes, such as chillies, grapes and cherries, and, using toothpicks, dip each piece first into an appropriate food colouring and then into the gelatine. Place on wax paper and chill slightly before serving.

GLOSSARY

BAMBOO SHOOTS

A cream-coloured, conical-shaped vegetable used frequently in all Asian cooking. When bought fresh and after removing the hard outer casing, they need boiling for a considerable time and it is much simpler to buy the canned variety which are readily available in all Asian provisions stores and many Western supermarkets.

BEAN SPROUTS

The sprouts of the green mung bean. Sold fresh in all Asian markets and are often found these days in Western supermarkets. May also be bought in cans.

BLACK MUSHROOMS

Also known as Chinese mushrooms. Sold dried and must be soaked in warm water for some time before using. The hard stems are nearly always discarded. The flavour is unique and really there is no acceptable substitute but they are readily available in even the smallest Asian provisions stores.

CHILLIES

Fresh chillies, of many varieties, play a major part in Thai cooking and the quantities used (despite what any recipe may suggest) must be a matter of personal taste. Special care should be taken with the very hot, small green chilli (*prik khee noo*), used liberally by the Thais but which often proves 'too

much' for the more tender foreign palate. With the larger red chillies, the 'fire' comes from the seeds and these should be discarded if a milder flavour is preferred. Dried chillies are more often used whole for cooking and discarded before serving.

COCONUT MILK

Where fresh coconuts are available, the milk is obtained by grating the flesh of a mature coconut and squeezing with water. On average, the flesh of 1 coconut squeezed with 75 ml water will produce the thick milk referred to most frequently. To make a thinner milk, the same process should be repeated one or more times. The liquid from young, green coconuts (often thought of as milk) is known as coconut water and is seldom used in Thai cooking. Where fresh coconuts are not available, the canned or frozen variety (preferably the latter) should be used.

CORIANDER

One of the most essential ingredients in Thai cooking. The seeds, roots and leaves are all used and each has its own distinctive flavour. Although part of the Western parsley family, this should not be thought of as a reasonable substitute. The seeds, of course, are readily available and the dried leaves and roots should be found in the better-stocked Asian provision stores.

CURRY LEAVES

Small, aromatic leaves which are best bought fresh. If not available and the dried variety are being used, adjust quantities accordingly.

GARLIC

The cloves of the Thai garlic are smaller than the Western variety but the taste differs hardly at all and there is no problem with substitution. The skins have a light pinkish tint and usually are not removed before chopping or crushing.

GLUTINOUS RICE

A long-grained variety of rice which, in spite of its name, is gluten-free. However, it becomes very sticky when cooked and is used frequently for rice desserts.

KAFFIR LIME

A local lime, somewhat larger than the type more familiar in Western countries. It has a dark green 'knobbly' skin with a sharp, aromatic flavour. The skin, juice and leaves are all used in Thai cooking and the first two are available dried. Lemons may be used as a reasonable substitute.

KHA

A Thai ginger root which is larger and whiter than the more universally known variety. It is seldom grown outside Southeast Asia but is available dried

in packages in some larger Asian provisions stores (and in Thai markets for those visiting the country) and will keep for very lengthy periods.

LEMON GRASS

An aromatic grass with a small bulbous root which, when crushed, gives a strong lemon flavour. When using the packaged powder form (serai) 1 teaspoon should be substituted for 1 stalk of fresh. As a very last resort, grated lemon peel can be used but, in one form or another, this is an essential ingredient of Thai cooking.

NAM PLA

A fish sauce, used as a seasoning and made, traditionally, by kneading tiny shrimps with salt and water and leaving in the sun for several days for the liquid to drip into a container. However, a more practical, and very acceptable, substitute can be made by blending 6 large anchovy fillets and 1 clove of garlic with 2 teaspoons of light soya sauce.

NAM PRIK

A spicy sauce often served as a side-dish. It is very strong, so care should be taken when using for the first time. Make by pounding together 2 tablespoons salted fish, 6 cloves garlic, 4 fresh red chillies, 25 ml Nam Pla (see above), 75 ml fresh lime juice, 2 teaspoons light soya sauce and 1/2 teaspoon palm sugar.

OYSTER SAUCE

Made from oysters boiled in salted water and soya sauce. Keeps well and adds a delicious extra flavour to meat and vegetable dishes.

PALM SUGAR

A strong flavoured sugar obtained from the sap of the Palmyra tree. After processing is usually sold in small slabs but is also available in cans. The flavour is distinctive but soft brown sugar makes a reasonable substitute.

PANDANUS LEAVES

The leaves may be used whole in the cooking and removed prior to serving or may be finely chopped and pounded with a little water to form a paste. Their use adds both flavour and colouring and, while there is no substitute for the distinctive flavour, a few drops of green colouring may be added when the leaves are not available.

PRESERVED SOYA BEANS

Available in cans. Very salty and should be well rinsed under cold running water for a few minutes before using.

SALTED FISH

Used occasionally in Thai cooking as well as being served as a side-dish. It should be thoroughly rinsed and then steamed for 30-40 minutes before storing. It is usually fried before use.

SHRIMP PASTE

A pungent paste made from dried shrimps. It adds a very distinctive flavour for which there is really no substitute. It is sold in small slabs, is readily available in Asian provisions stores and can be kept for lengthy periods in an air-tight container.

SWEET BASIL

A strong and pungent herb used frequently in Thai cooking. Not always easy to find fresh but readily available in a dried form or preserved in oil.

TAMARIND WATER

Made by soaking fresh or dried tamarind rind in cold water for 15-20 minutes, then straining the liquid through a fine sieve. It adds a very distinctive sour taste and should only be used in small quantities.

INGREDIENTS (English/*Thai*)

BANANA/*GLUAY*
BALSAM LEAVES/*BAI KAPROW*
BASIL LEAVES/*BAI HORABHA*
BAY LEAVES/*BAI KRAWAN*
BEAN CURD/*TAO HOO*
BEANSPROUTS/*THUA NGOK*
BEEF/*NEAU*
CARDAMON/*LOOG KRAWAN*
CHILLIES/*PRIG*
CINNAMON/*OHB CHOEY*
CHICKEN/*GAI*
CLOVES/*KAAN PLOO*
COCONUT/*MA PROW*
CORIANDER/*PAAK CHEE*
CUMIN/*YEERA*
CUSTARD APPLE/*NOI NA*
CUCUMBER/*TAENG KWA*
DRIED FISH/*PLA HAENG*
DRIED BLACK MUSHROOMS/*HED HOM*
DRIED PRAWNS/*GOONG HAENG*

EGG NOODLES/*BA MEE*
EGGPLANT/*MA KHUEA*
FISH/*PLA*
FISH SAUCE/*NAAM PLA*
GARLIC/*KRA THIAM*
GINGER/*KHING*
GRAPES/*ANGOON*
GUAVA/*FARANG*
JACKFRUIT/*KHA NOON*
JELLY NOODLES/*WOON SEE*
KAFFIR LIME/*MA KROOD*
LEMON GRASS/*TA KRAI*
LYCHEE/*LINCHEE*
MANGO/*MA MUANG*
MANGOSTEEN/*MUNG KOOD*
MINT LEAVES/*BAI SARANAE*
MUSHROOMS/*HED*
NUTMEG/*LOOG CHAND*
ORANGE/*SOM*
PALM SUGAR/*NAAM TAAN PEEP*

PANDANUS LEAVES/*BAI TOEY*
PAPAYA/*MALA KAW*
PEPPER/*PRIG THAI*
PORK/*MOO*
PRAWNS/*GOONG*
PUMPKIN/*FUG THONG*
RAMBUTANS/*NGAW*
RICE/*KHOW*
RICE NOODLES/*GUAY TIAW*
RICE VERMICELLI/*SEN MEE*
SESAME/*NGA*
SHALLOTS/*HORM LEK*
SIAMESE GINGER/*KHA*
TAMARIND/*MAAK KAM*
TURMERIC/*KHA MIN*
WATER CHESTNUT/*HAEW*
WATER SPINACH/*PAK BOONG*
WHITE RADISH/*HUA PAKKAD*
WINTER MELON/*FUG*